This Brain Dump
JOURNAL
BELONGS TO:
....

Dedication

This Brain Dump Journal is dedicated to all the people out there who want to get all their thoughts out of their head and down on paper, and document their findings in the process.

You are my inspiration for producing books and I'm honored to be a part of keeping all of your Brain Dump notes, and records organized.

This journal notebook will help you record your details about tracking your thoughts in your head.

Thoughtfully put together with these sections to record: Stop Stressing About, Ideas, Things To Do, Conversations, Shopping List, Exploe & Learn About, & Blank Lined Journal Pages.

How to Use this Book

The purpose of this book is to keep all of your Brain Dump notes all in one place. It will help keep you organized.

This Brain Dump Journal Book will allow you to accurately document every detail about all of the thoughts & ideas swimming around in your head. It's a great way to chart your course by getting it all down on paper.

Here are examples of the prompts for you to fill in and write about your experience in this book:

1. Stop Stressing About
2. Ideas
3. Things To Do
4. Conversations
5. Shopping List
6. Explore & Learn About
7. Blank Lined Journal Pages

Stop stressing about...

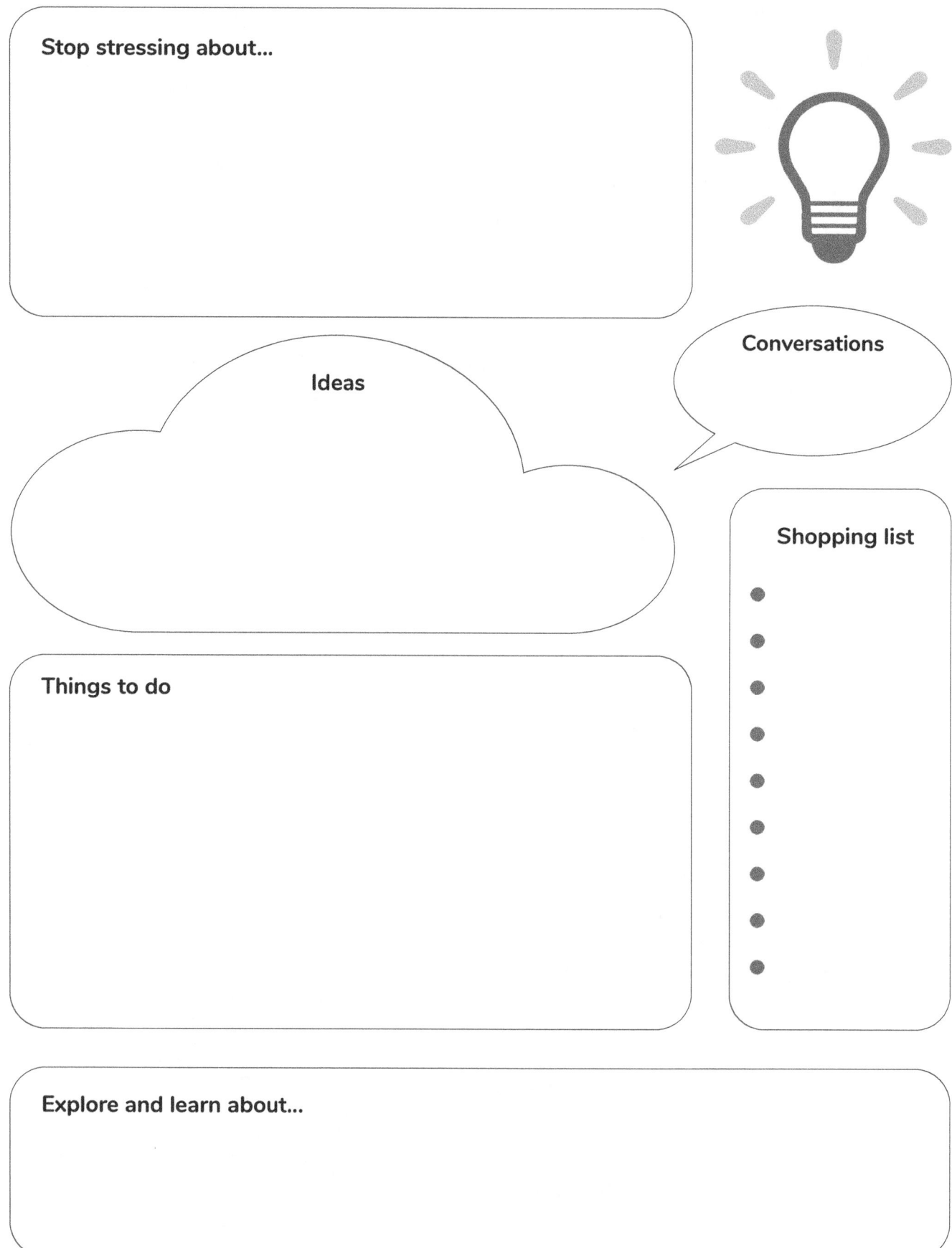

Ideas

Conversations

Things to do

Shopping list

Explore and learn about...

Stop stressing about...

Ideas

Conversations

Shopping list
-
-
-
-
-
-
-
-
-

Things to do

Explore and learn about...

Stop stressing about...

Ideas

Conversations

Things to do

Shopping list
-
-
-
-
-
-
-
-
-

Explore and learn about...

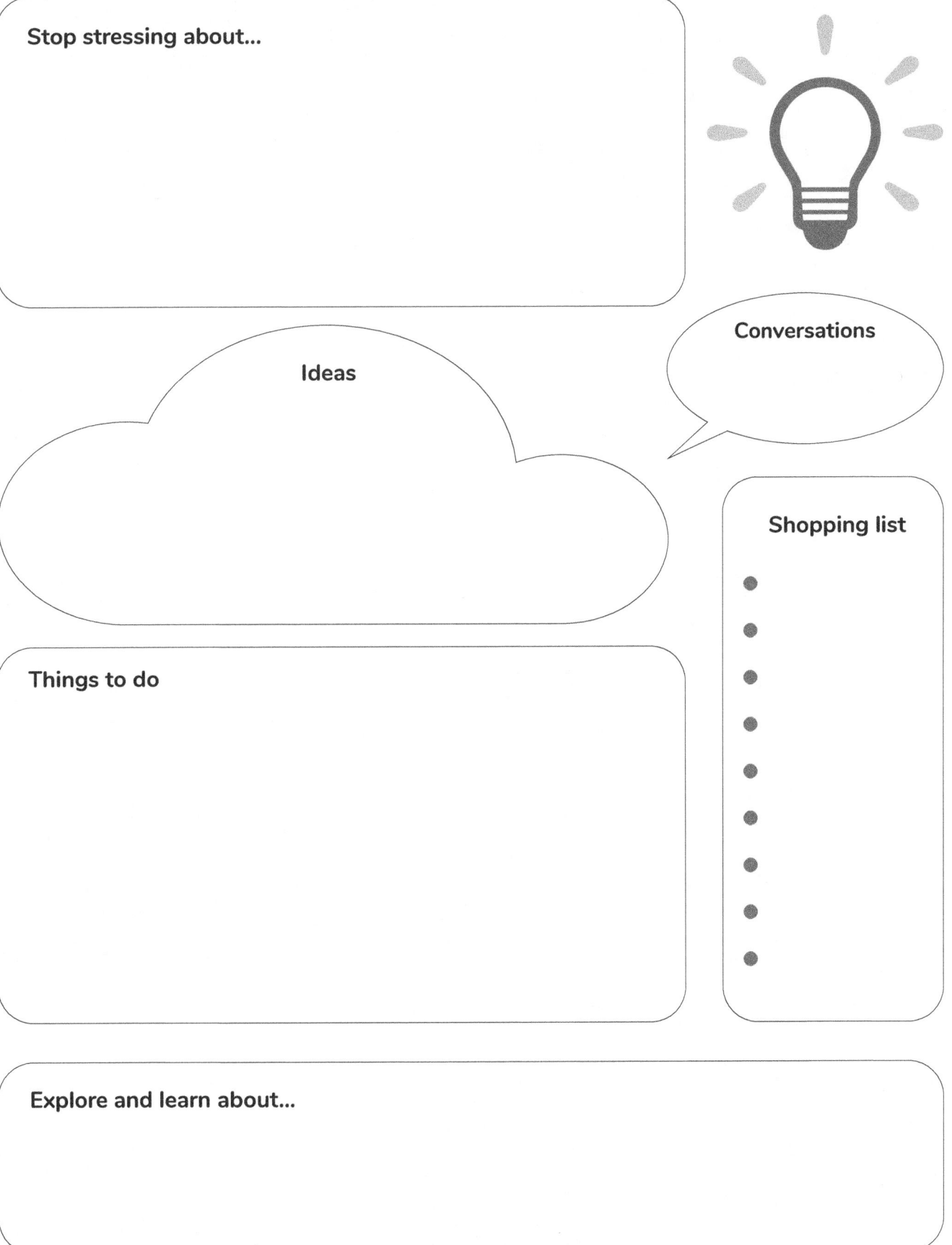

Stop stressing about...

Ideas

Conversations

Shopping list
-
-
-
-
-
-
-
-
-
-

Things to do

Explore and learn about...

Stop stressing about...

Ideas

Conversations

Shopping list
-
-
-
-
-
-
-
-
-

Things to do

Explore and learn about...

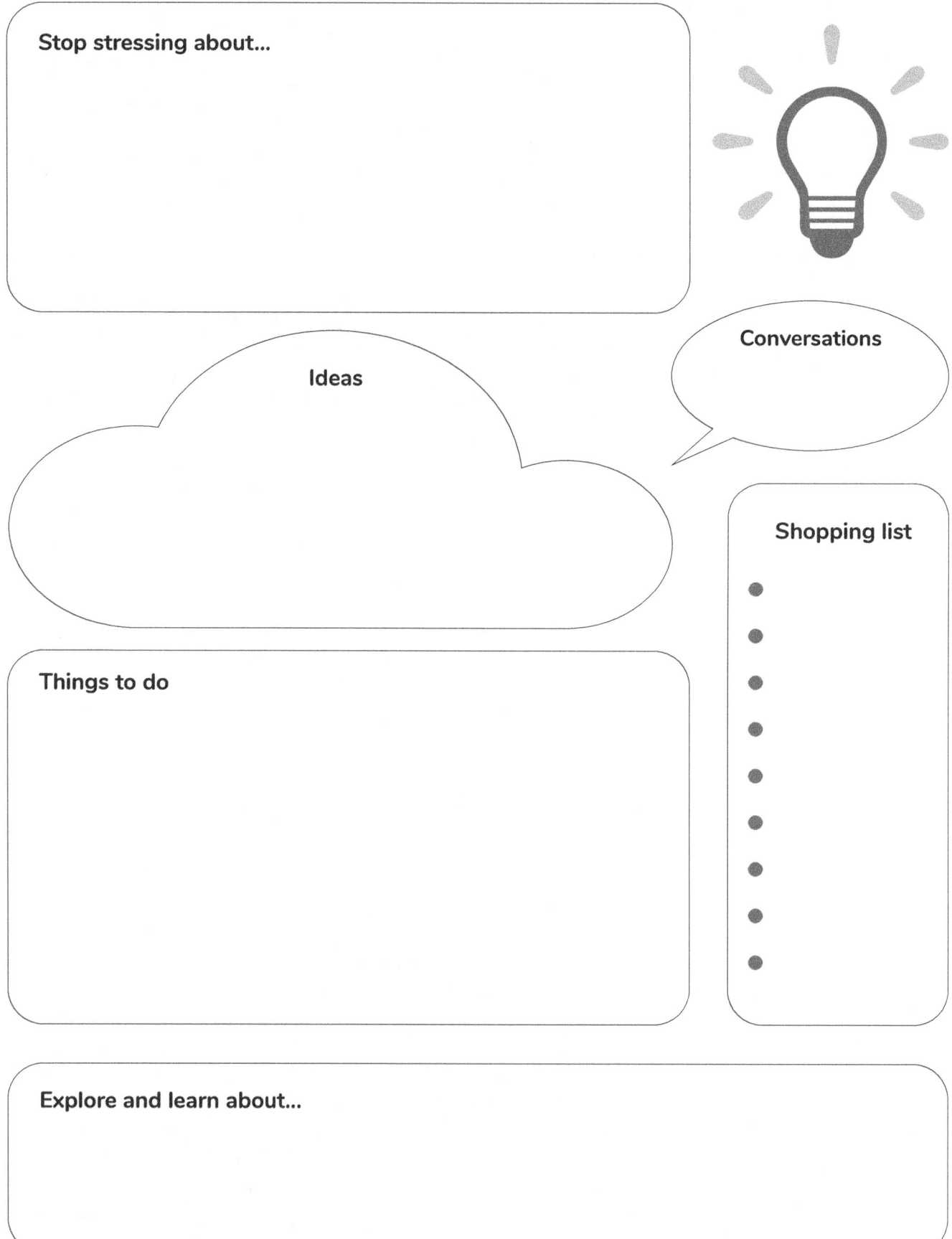

Stop stressing about...

Ideas

Conversations

Shopping list
-
-
-
-
-
-
-
-
-

Things to do

Explore and learn about...

Stop stressing about...

Ideas

Conversations

Things to do

Shopping list
-
-
-
-
-
-
-
-
-

Explore and learn about...

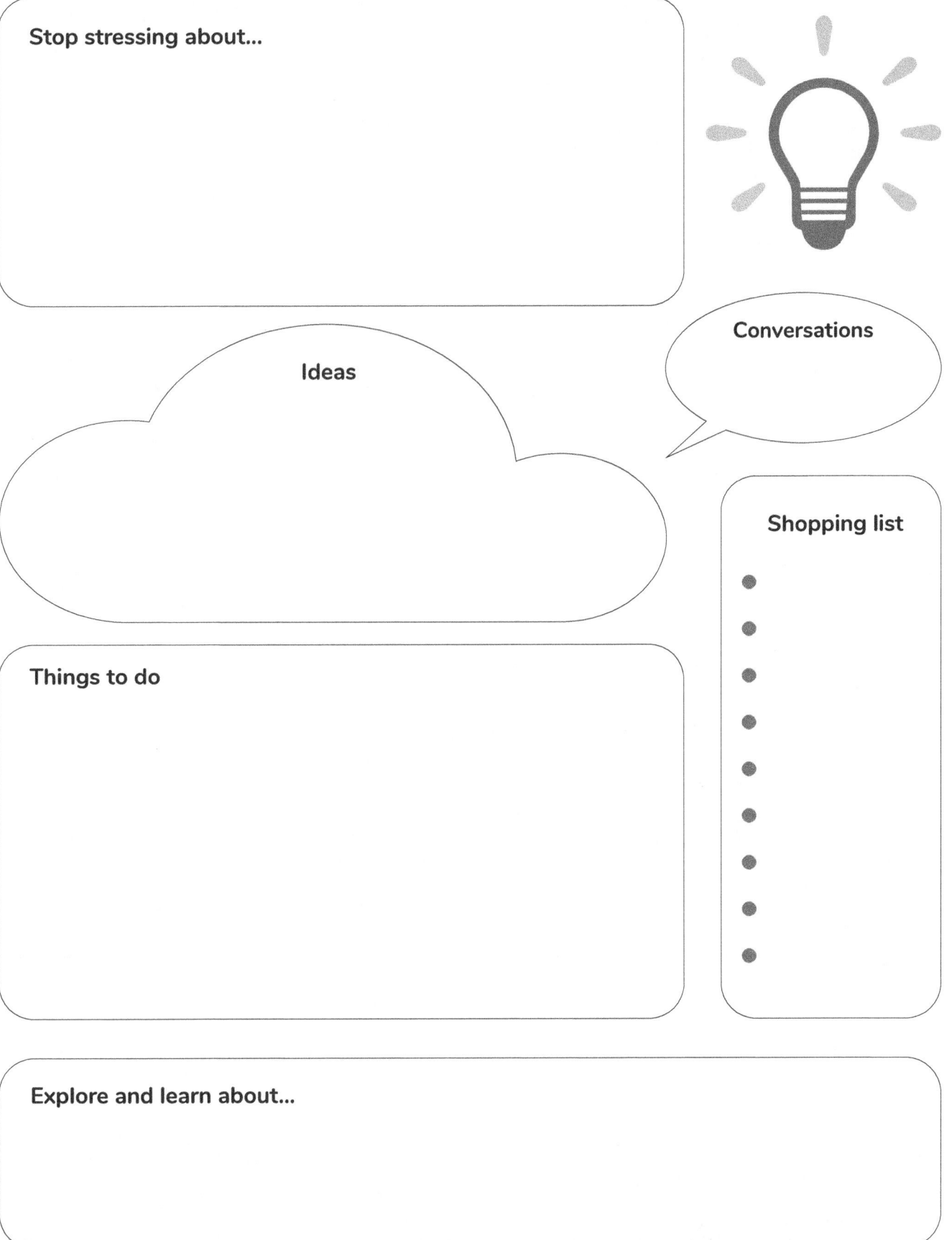

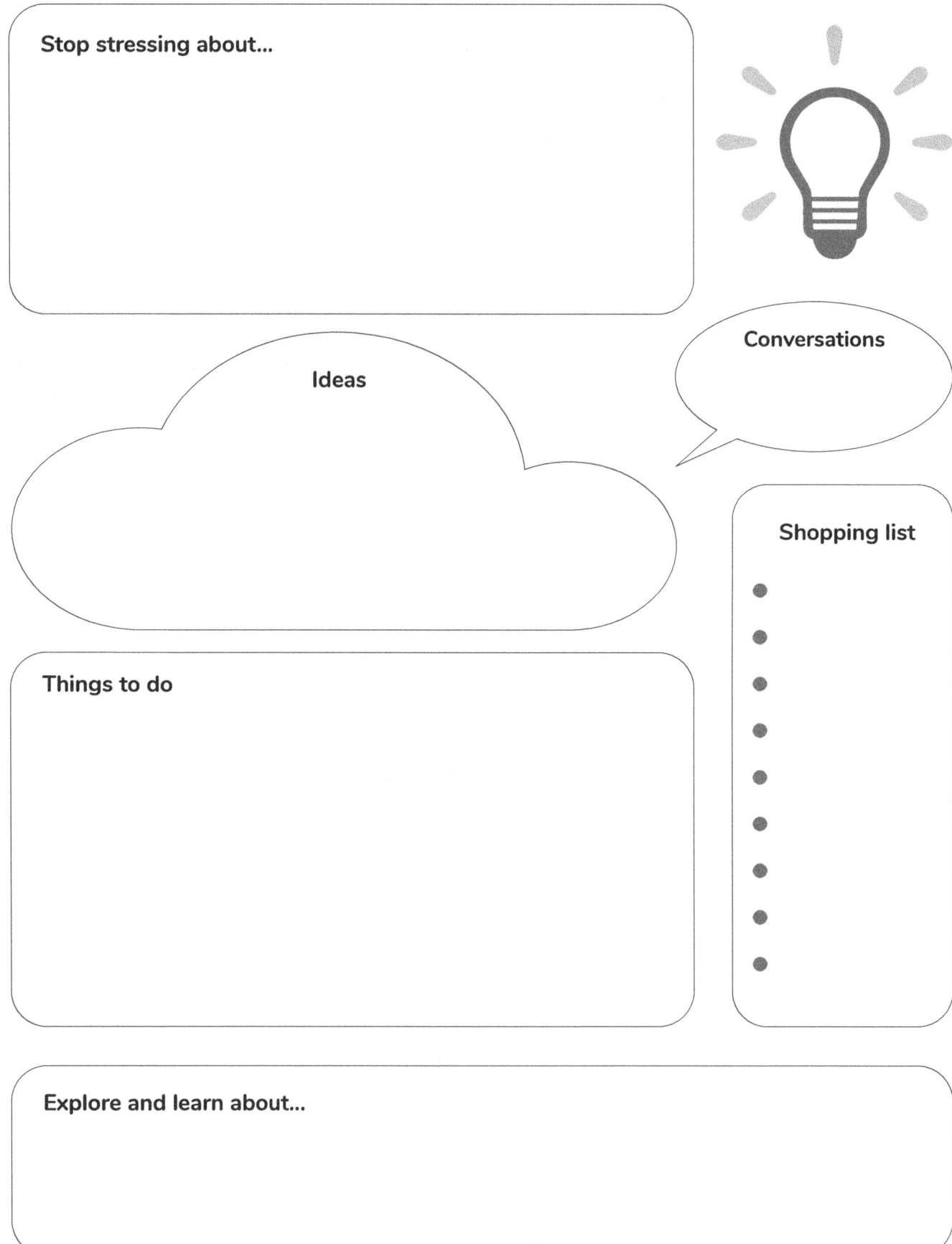

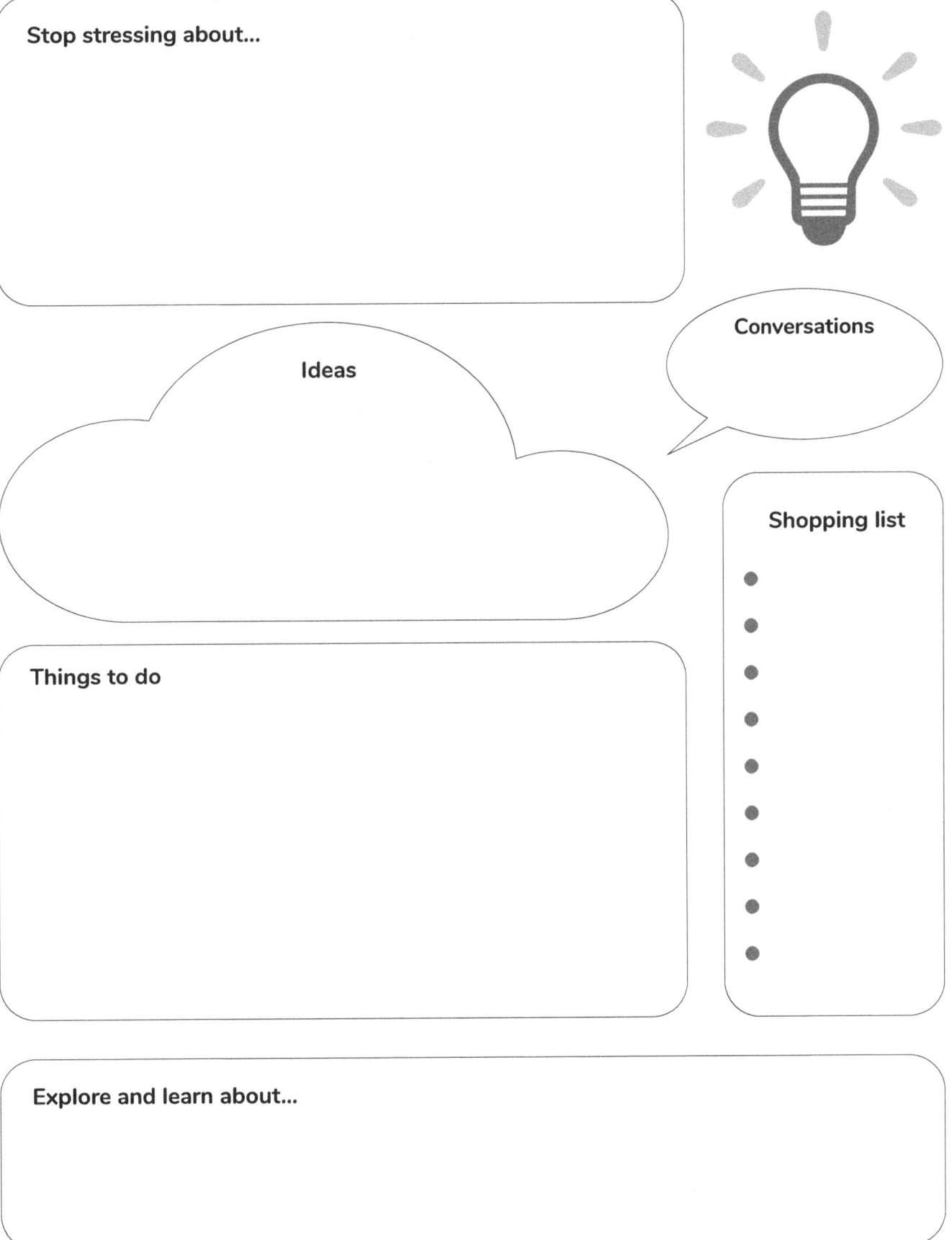

Stop stressing about...

Ideas

Conversations

Shopping list
-
-
-
-
-
-
-
-
-
-

Things to do

Explore and learn about...

Stop stressing about...

Ideas

Conversations

Shopping list
-
-
-
-
-
-
-
-
-

Things to do

Explore and learn about...

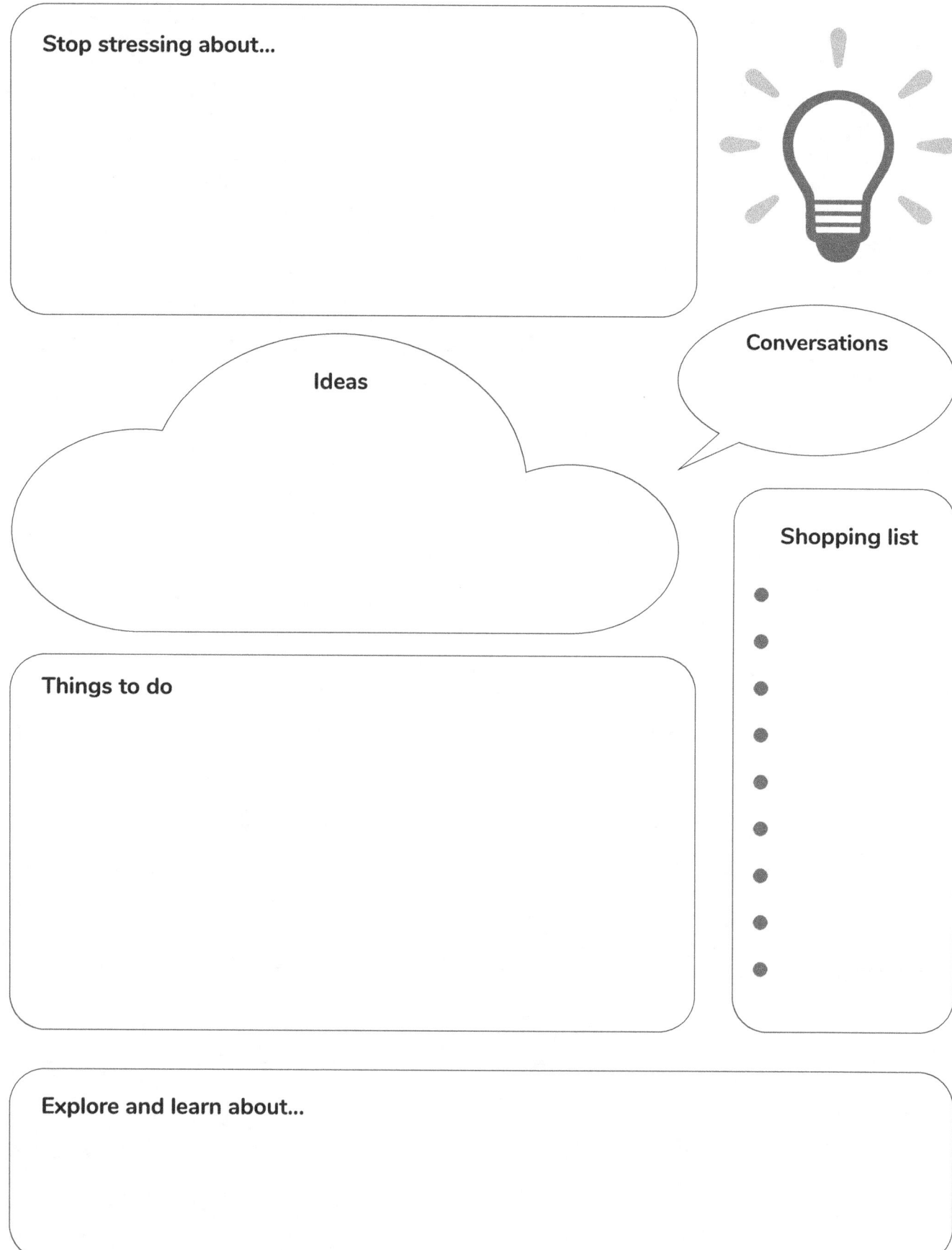

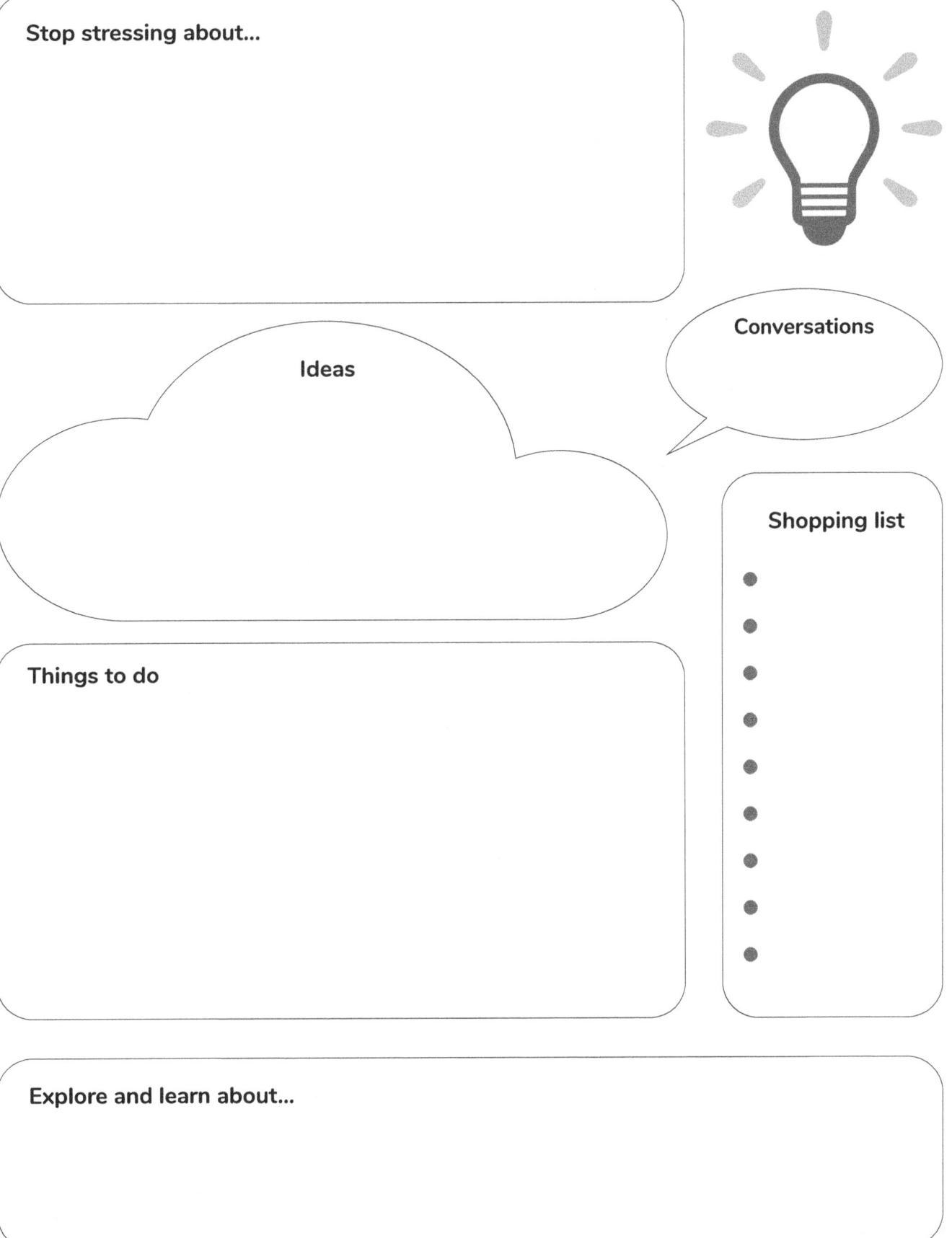

Stop stressing about...

Ideas

Conversations

Shopping list
-
-
-
-
-
-
-
-
-

Things to do

Explore and learn about...

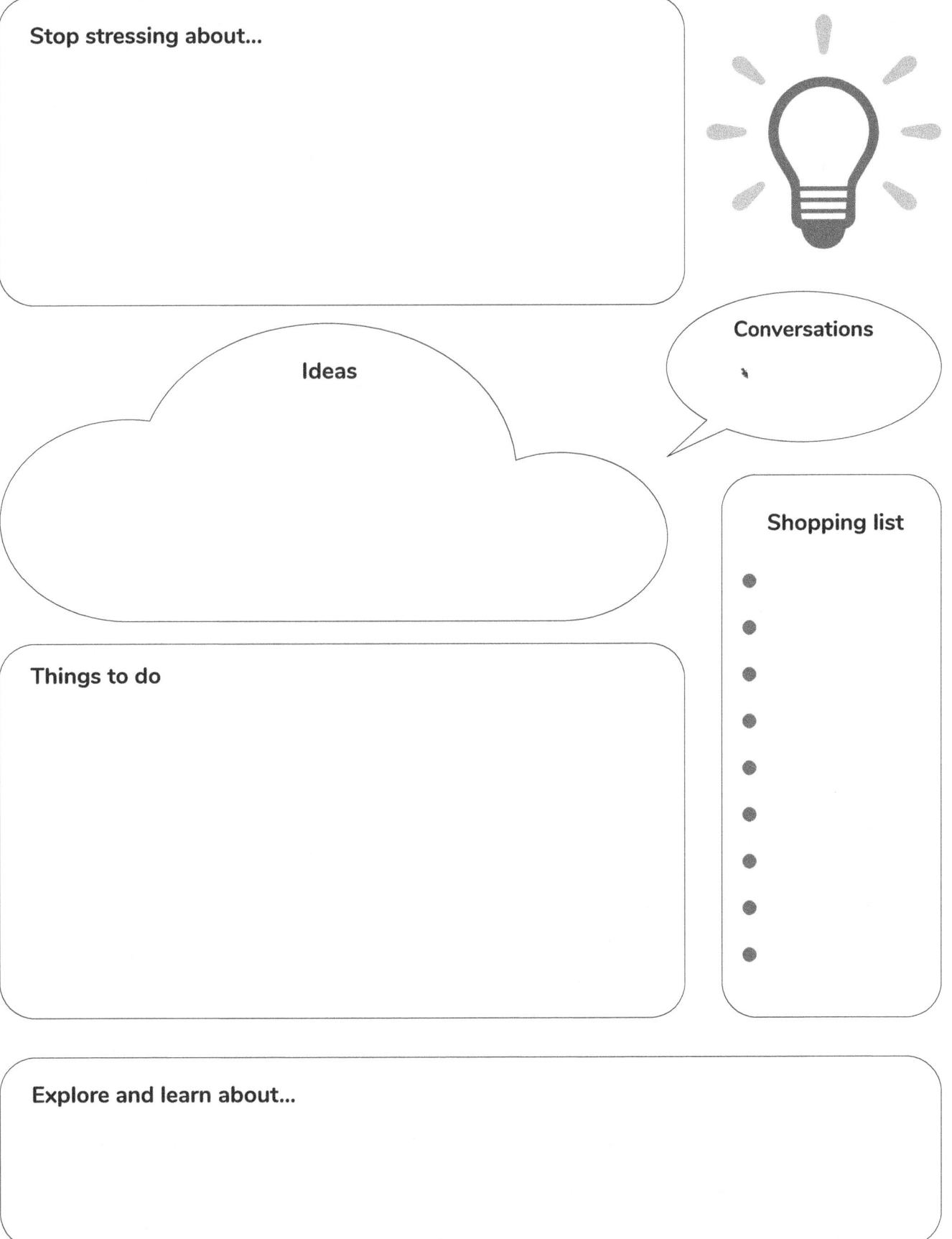

Stop stressing about...

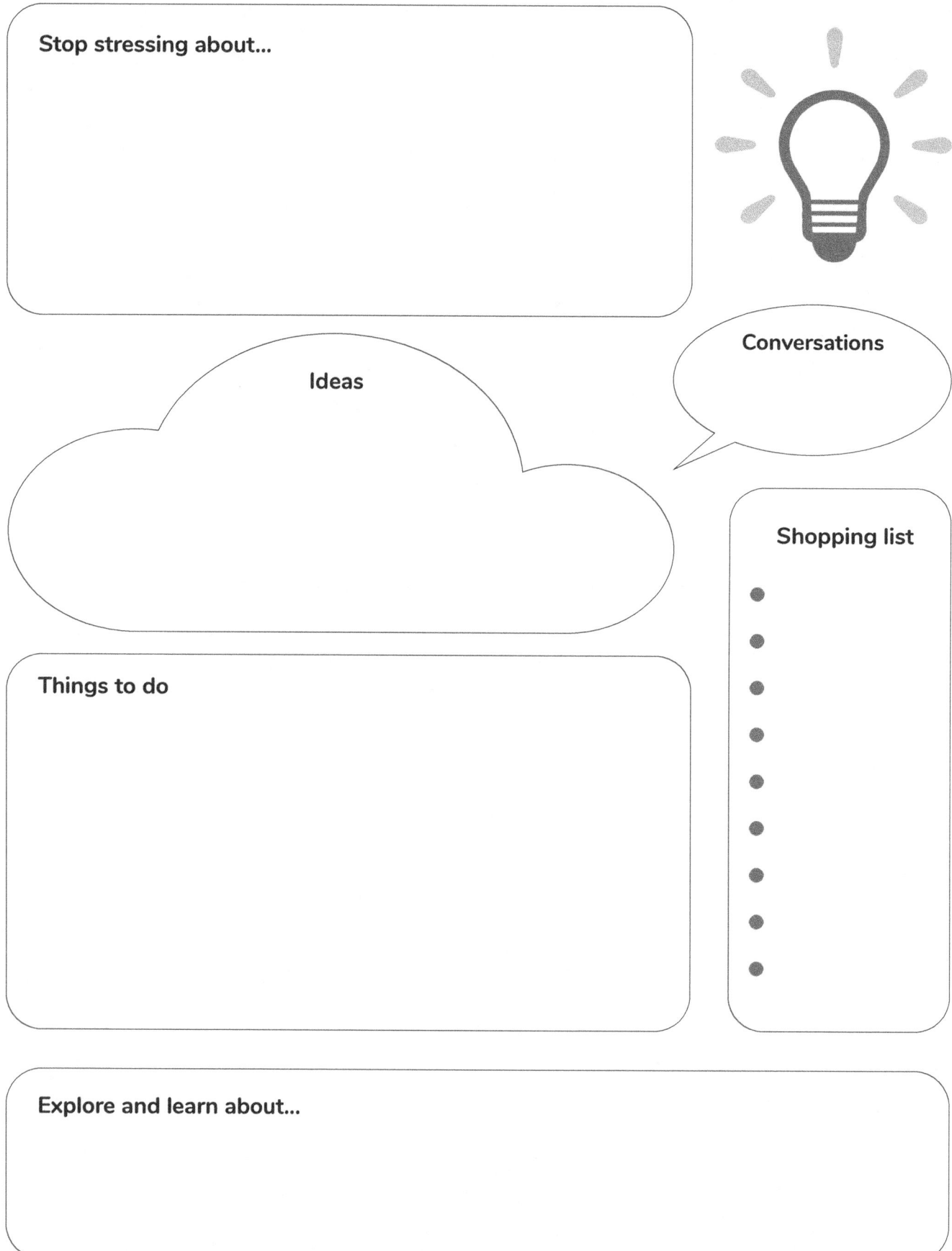

Ideas

Conversations

Shopping list
-
-
-
-
-
-
-
-
-

Things to do

Explore and learn about...

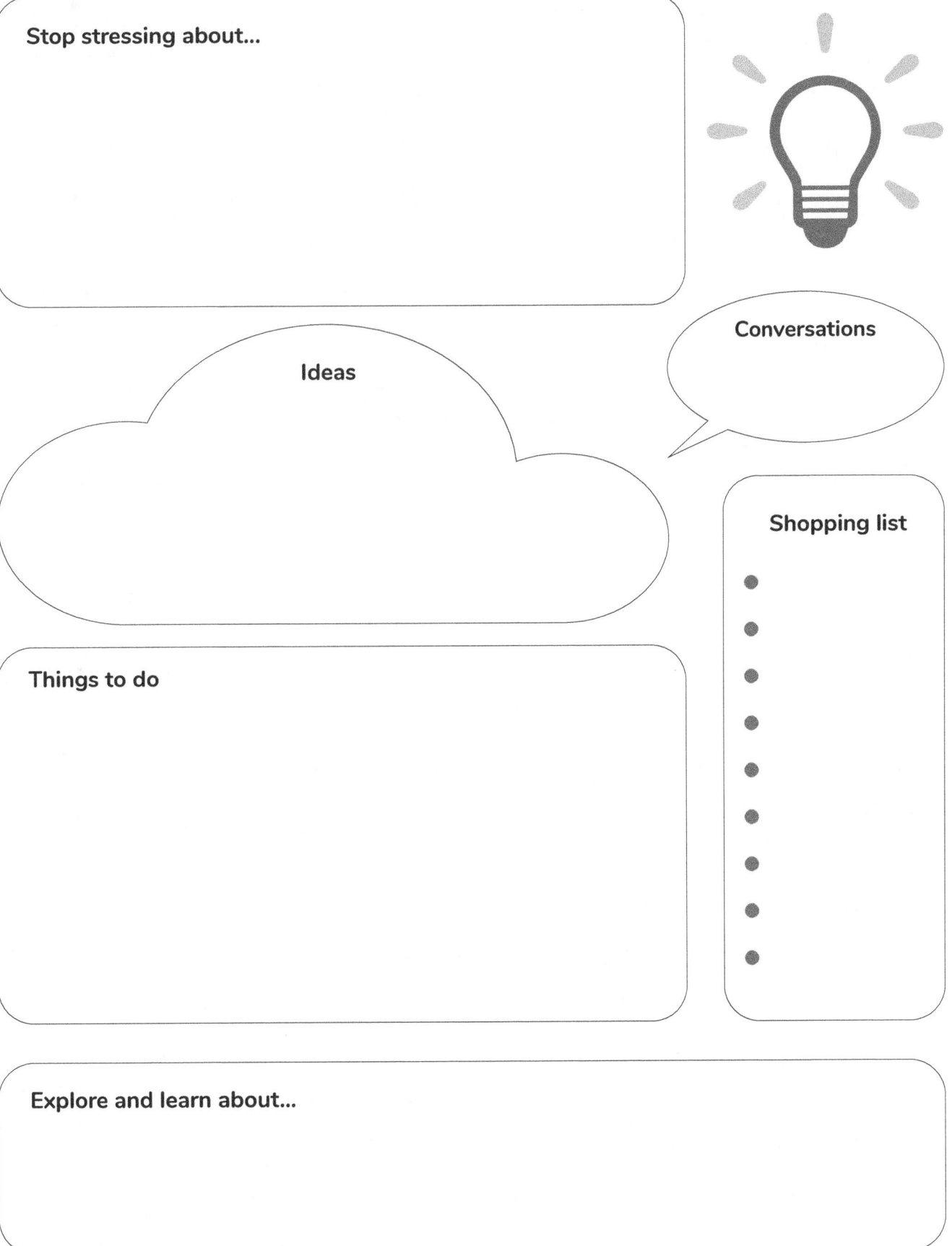

Stop stressing about...

Ideas

Conversations

Shopping list
-
-
-
-
-
-
-
-
-
-

Things to do

Explore and learn about...

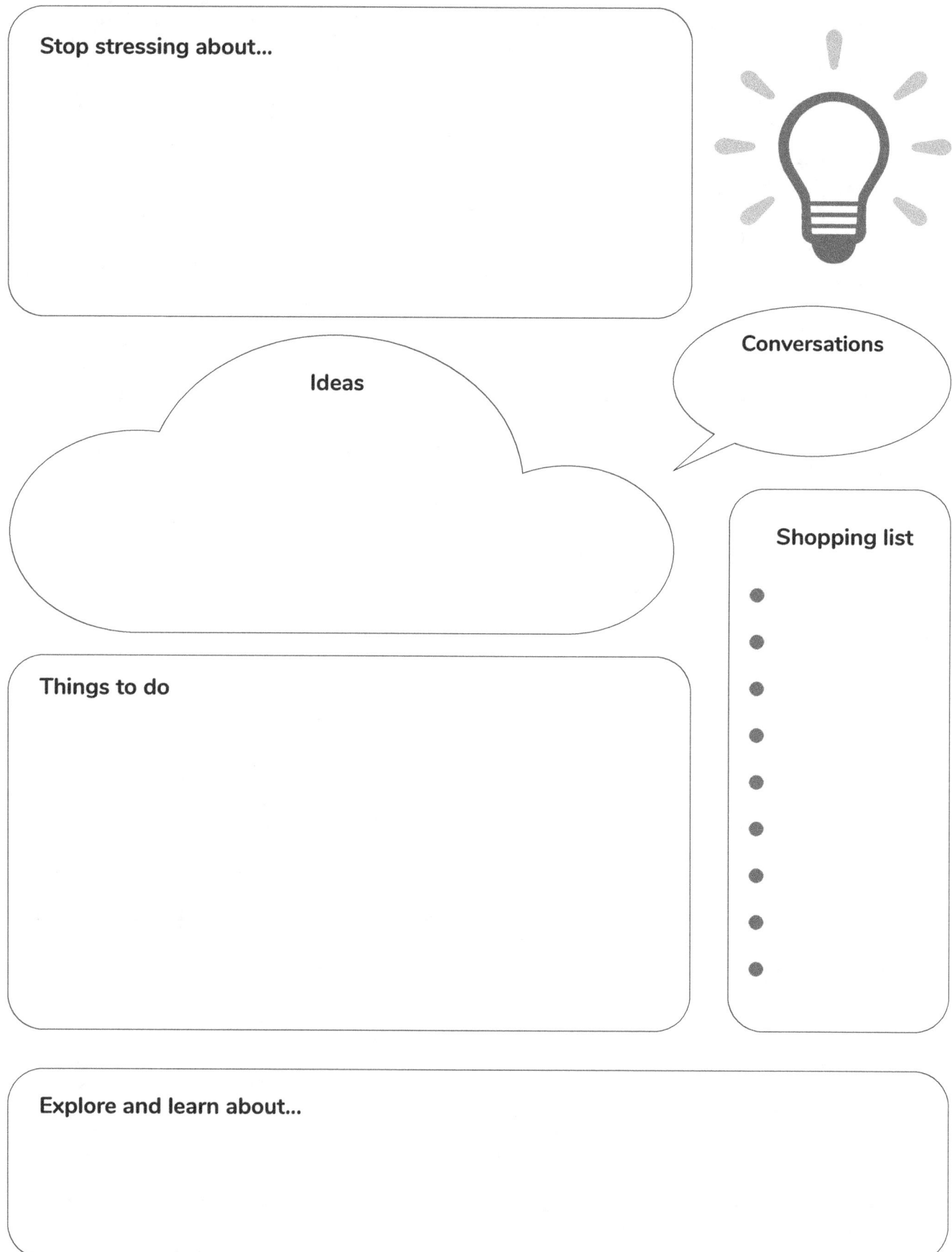

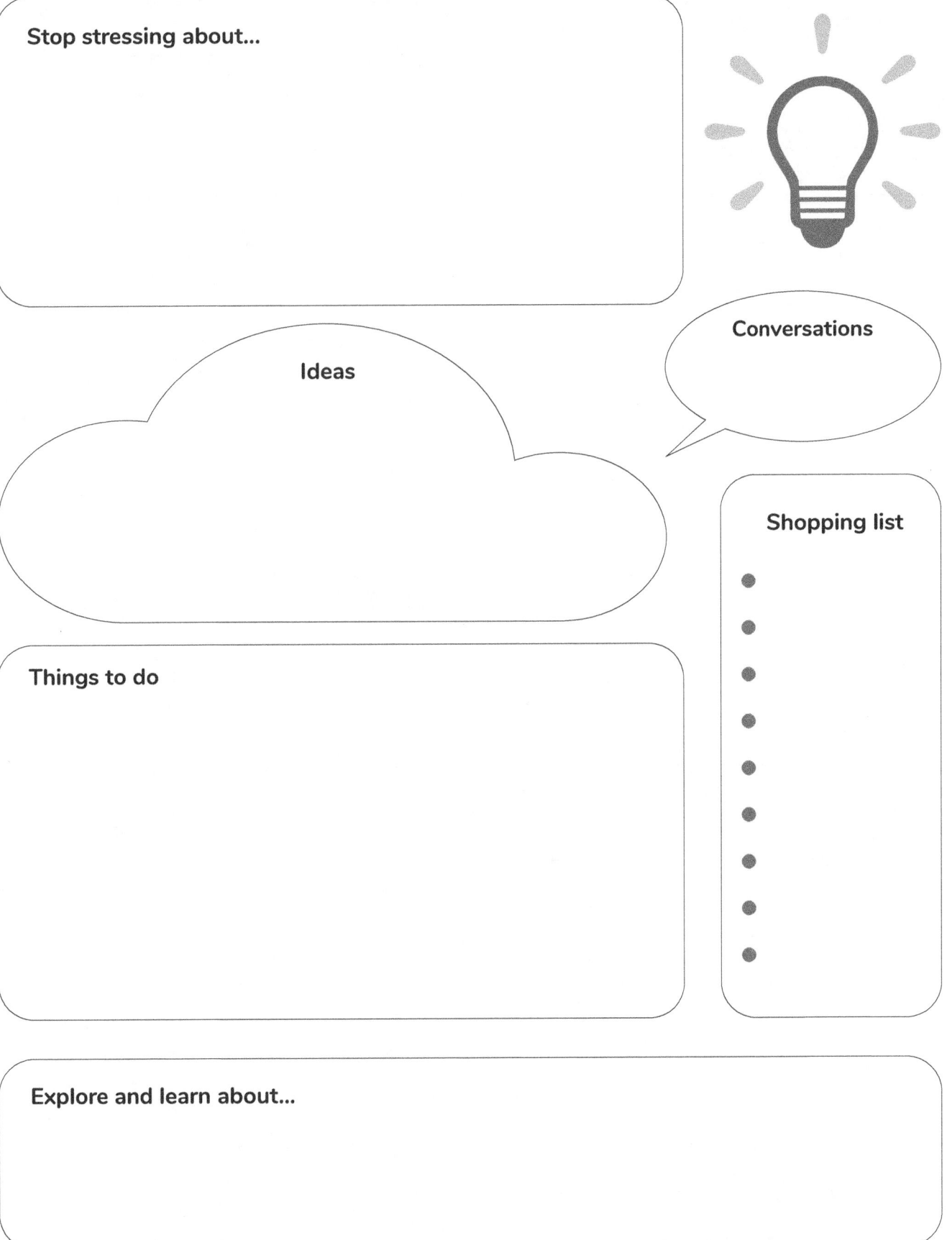

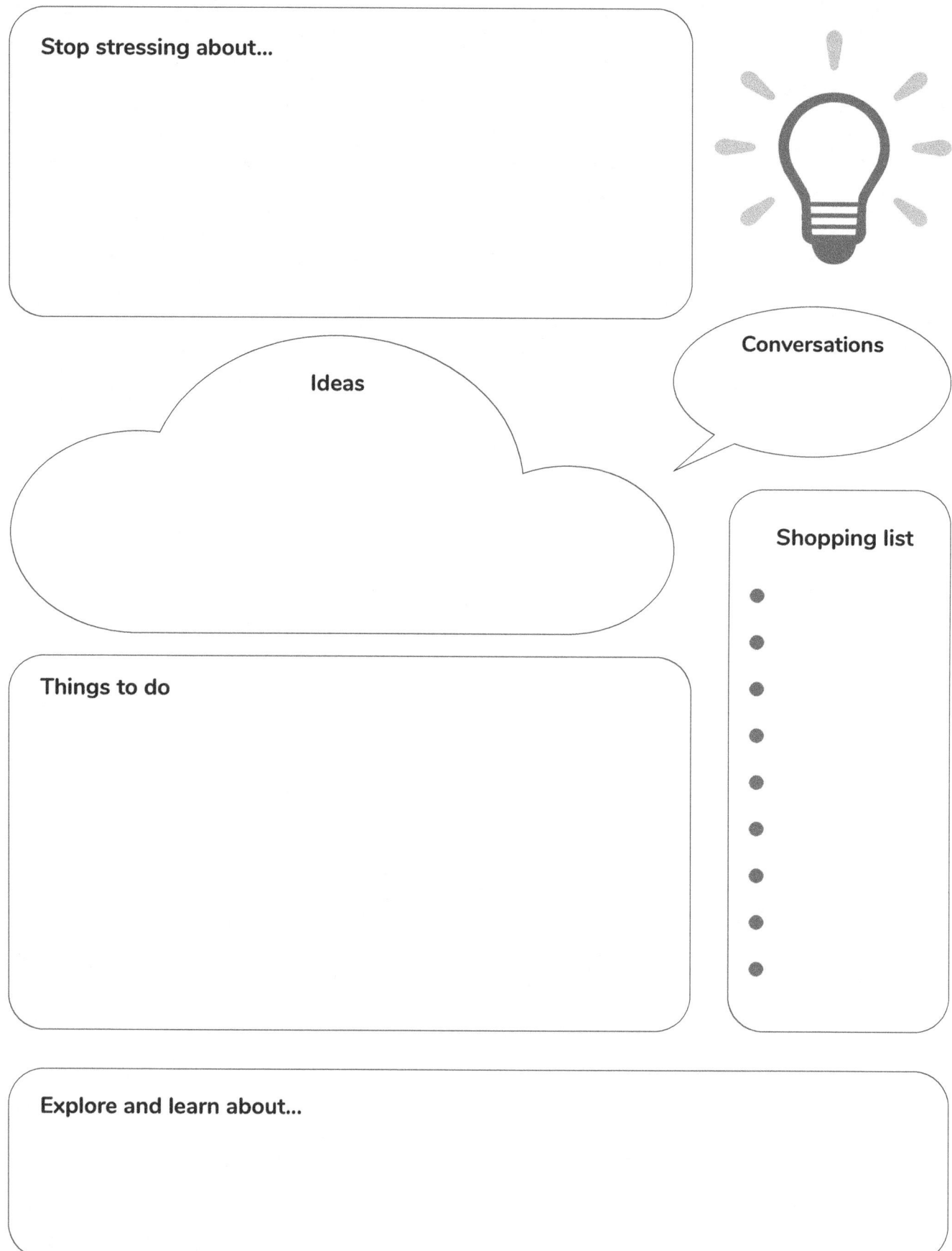

Stop stressing about...

Ideas

Conversations

Things to do

Shopping list
-
-
-
-
-
-
-
-
-

Explore and learn about...

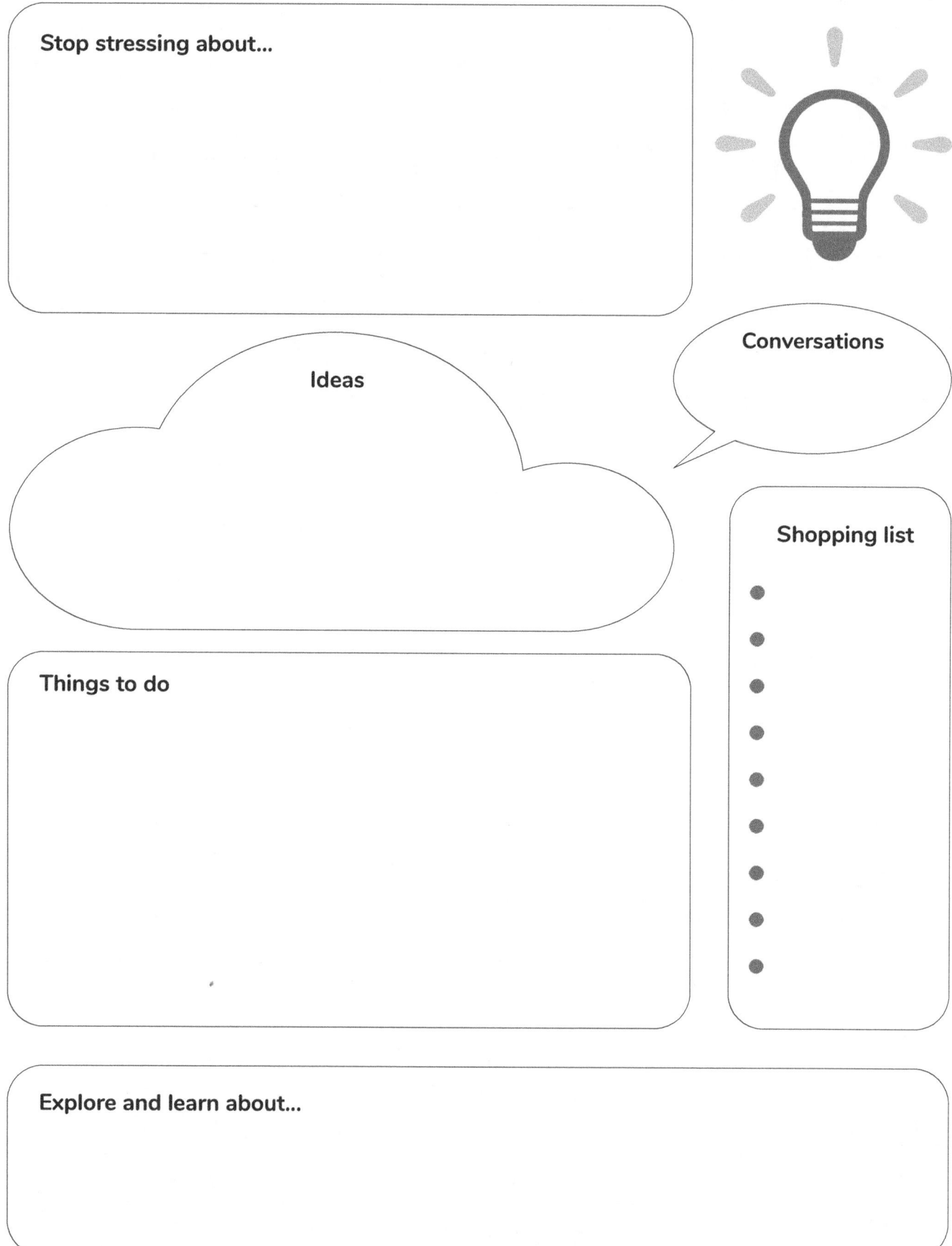

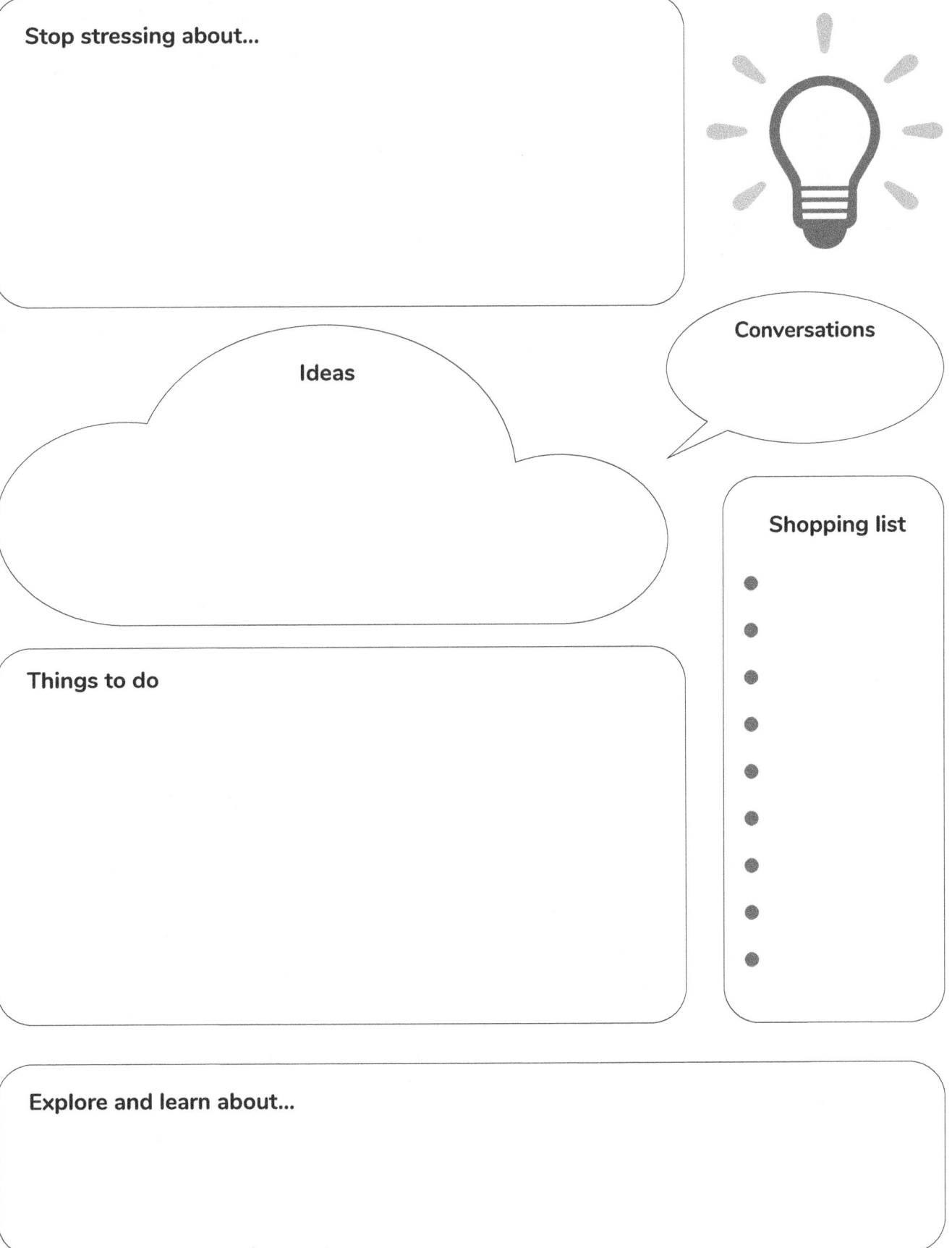

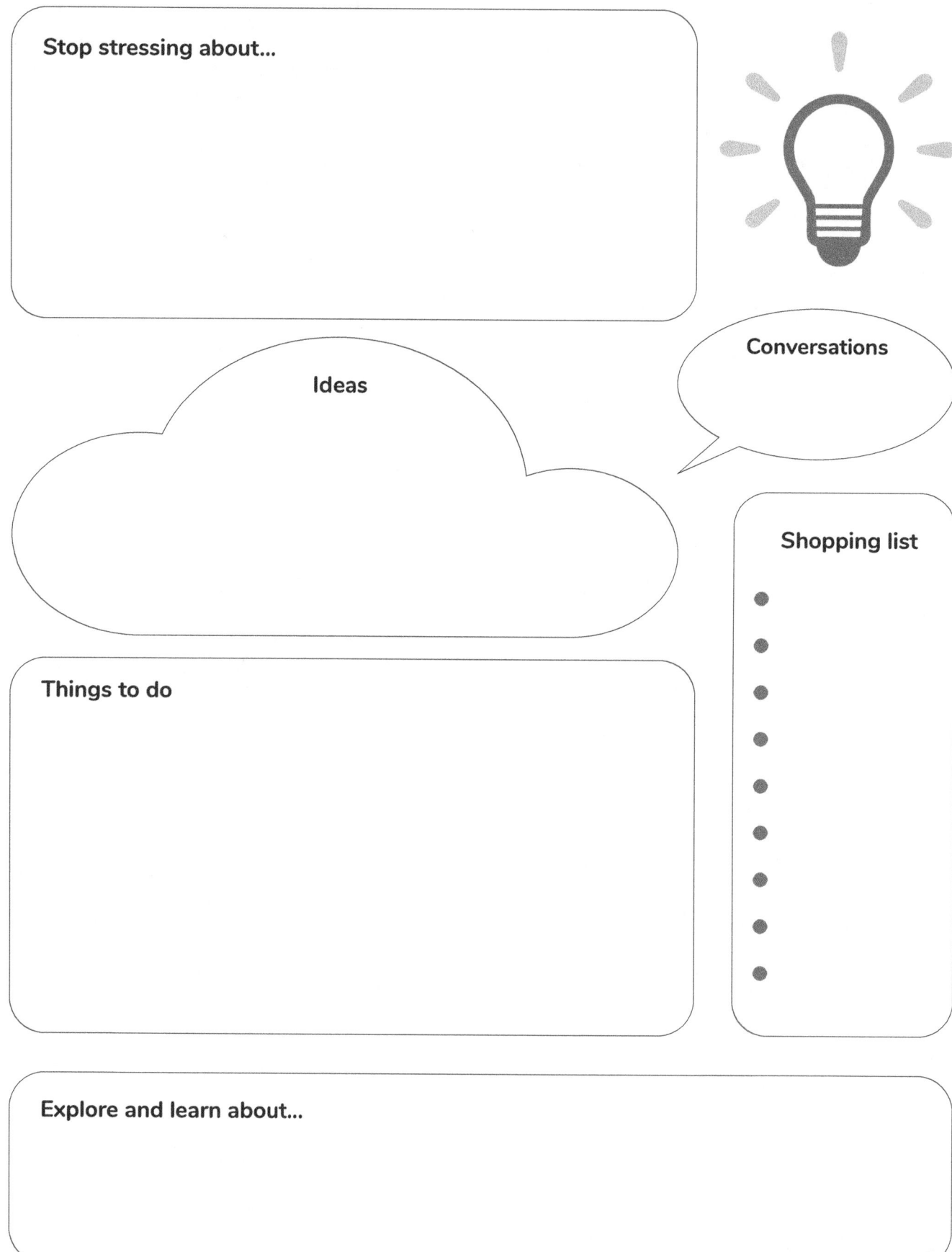

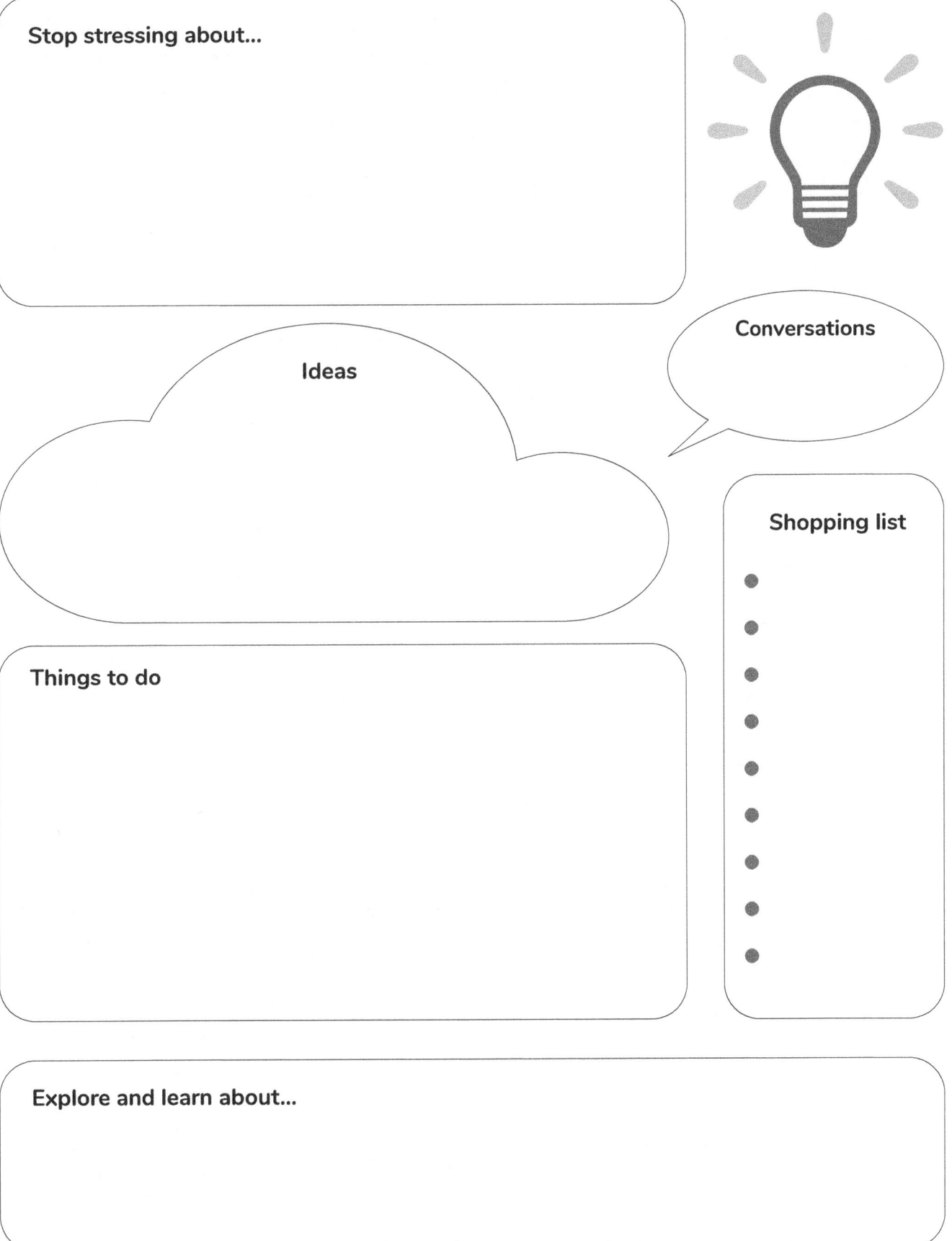

Stop stressing about...

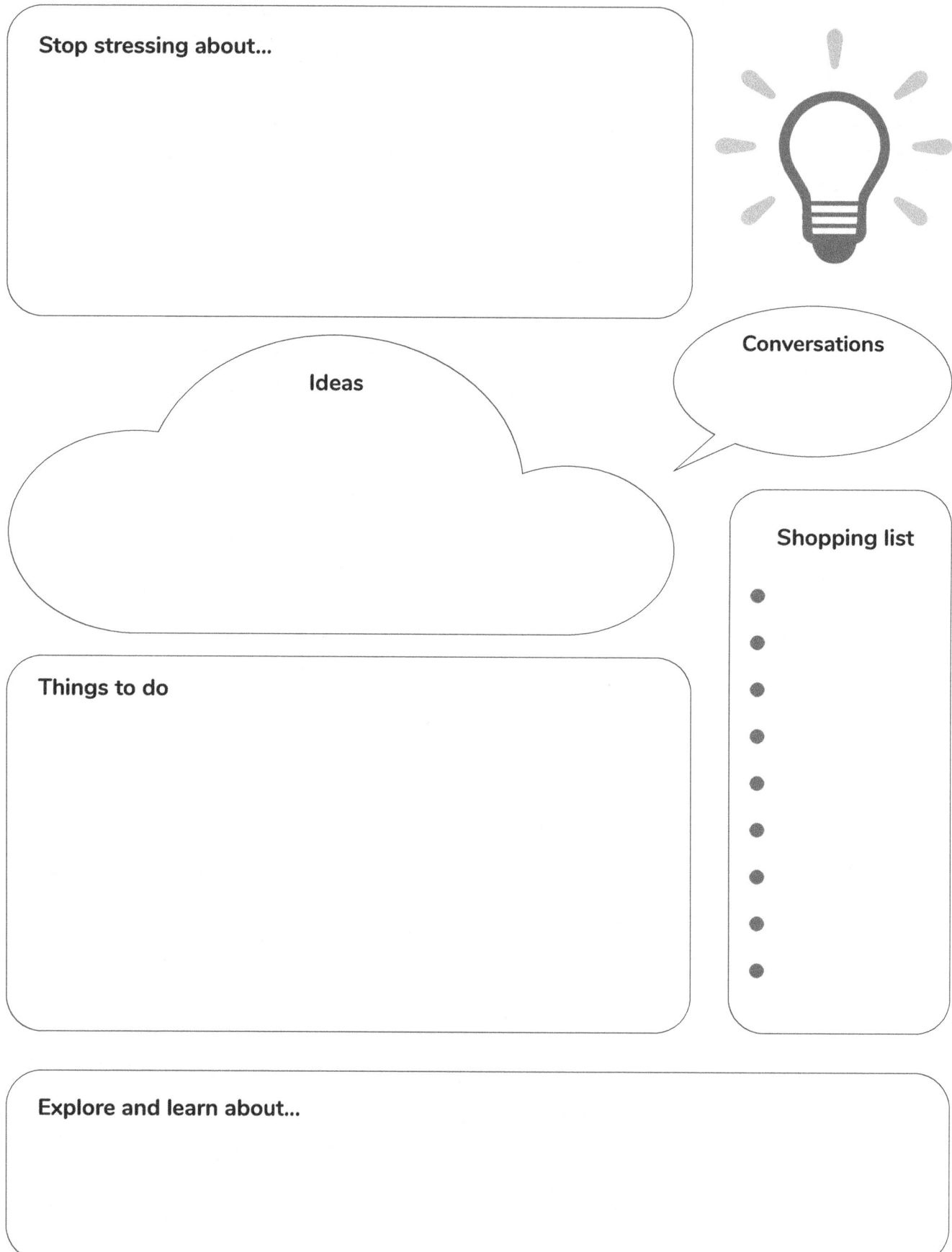

Ideas

Conversations

Things to do

Shopping list
-
-
-
-
-
-
-
-
-

Explore and learn about...

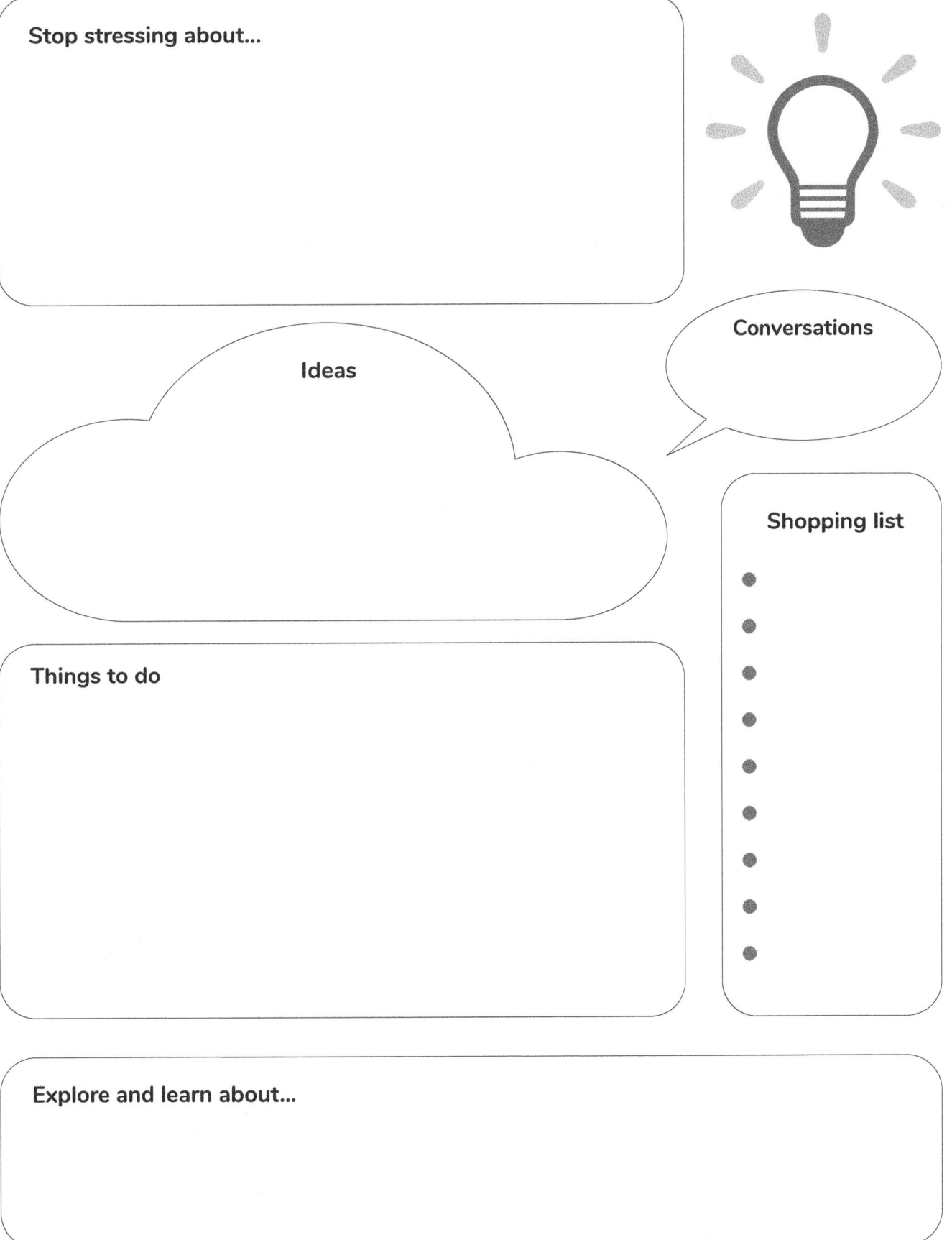

Stop stressing about...

Ideas

Conversations

Shopping list
-
-
-
-
-
-
-
-
-

Things to do

Explore and learn about...

Stop stressing about...

Ideas

Conversations

Shopping list
-
-
-
-
-
-
-
-
-

Things to do

Explore and learn about...

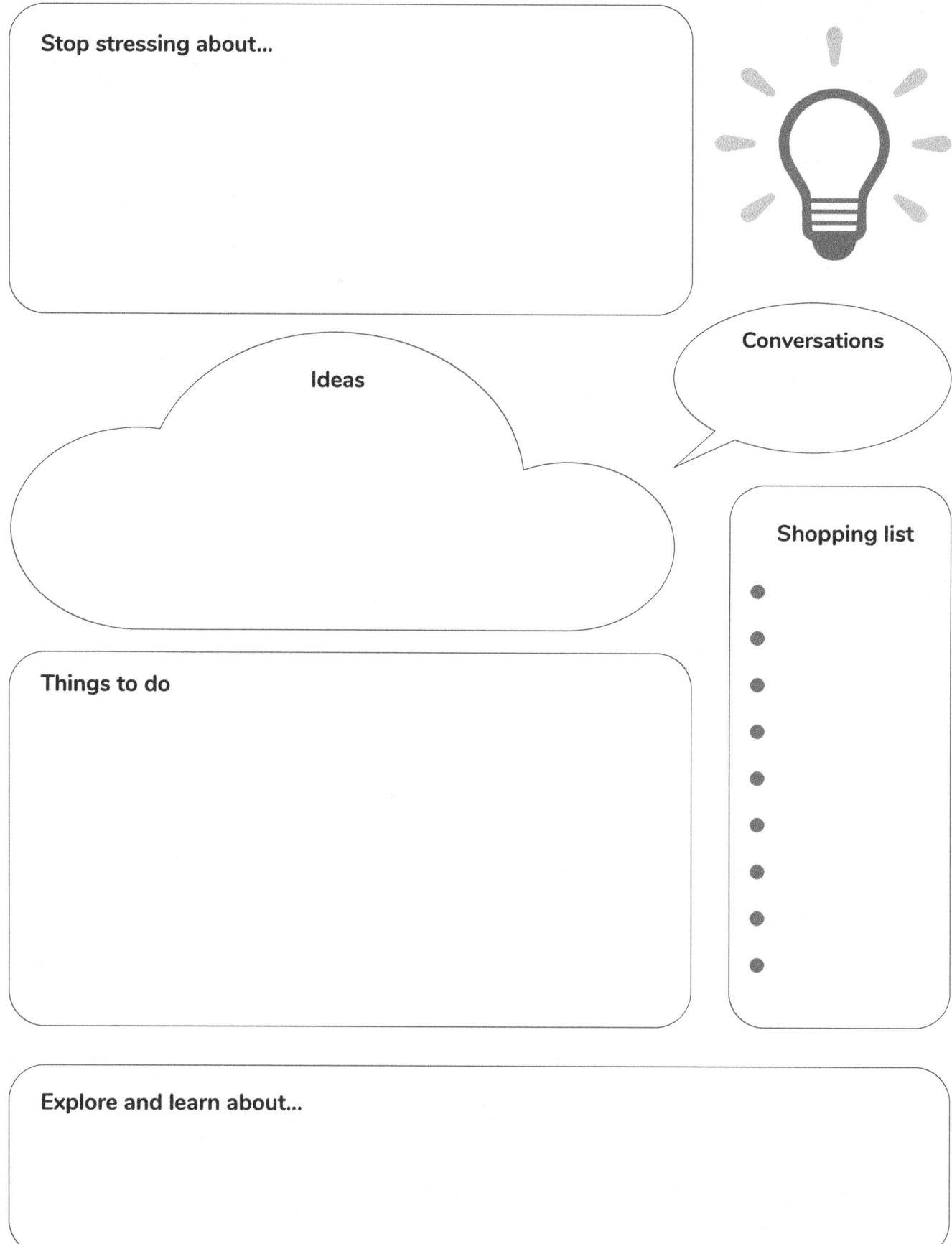

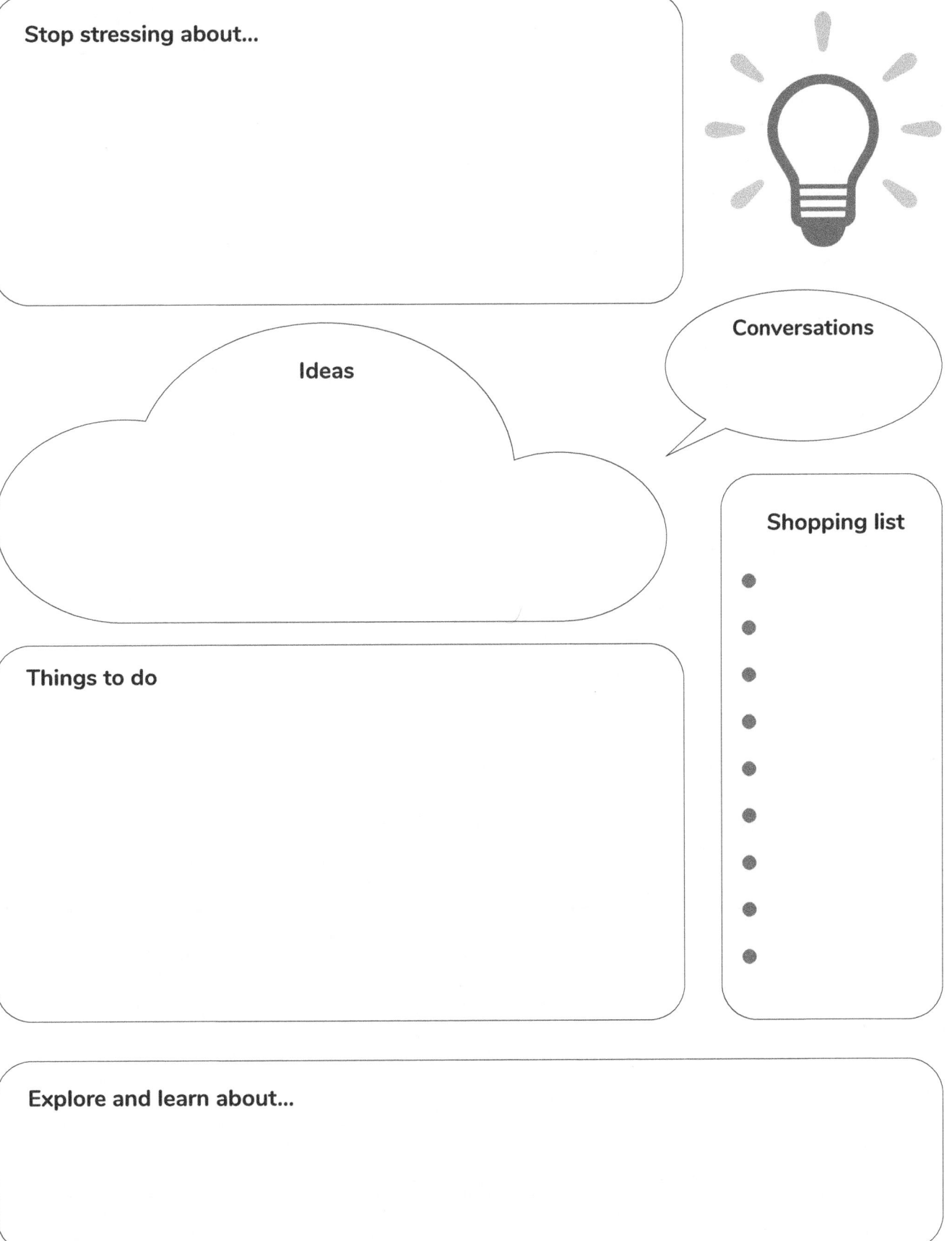

Stop stressing about...

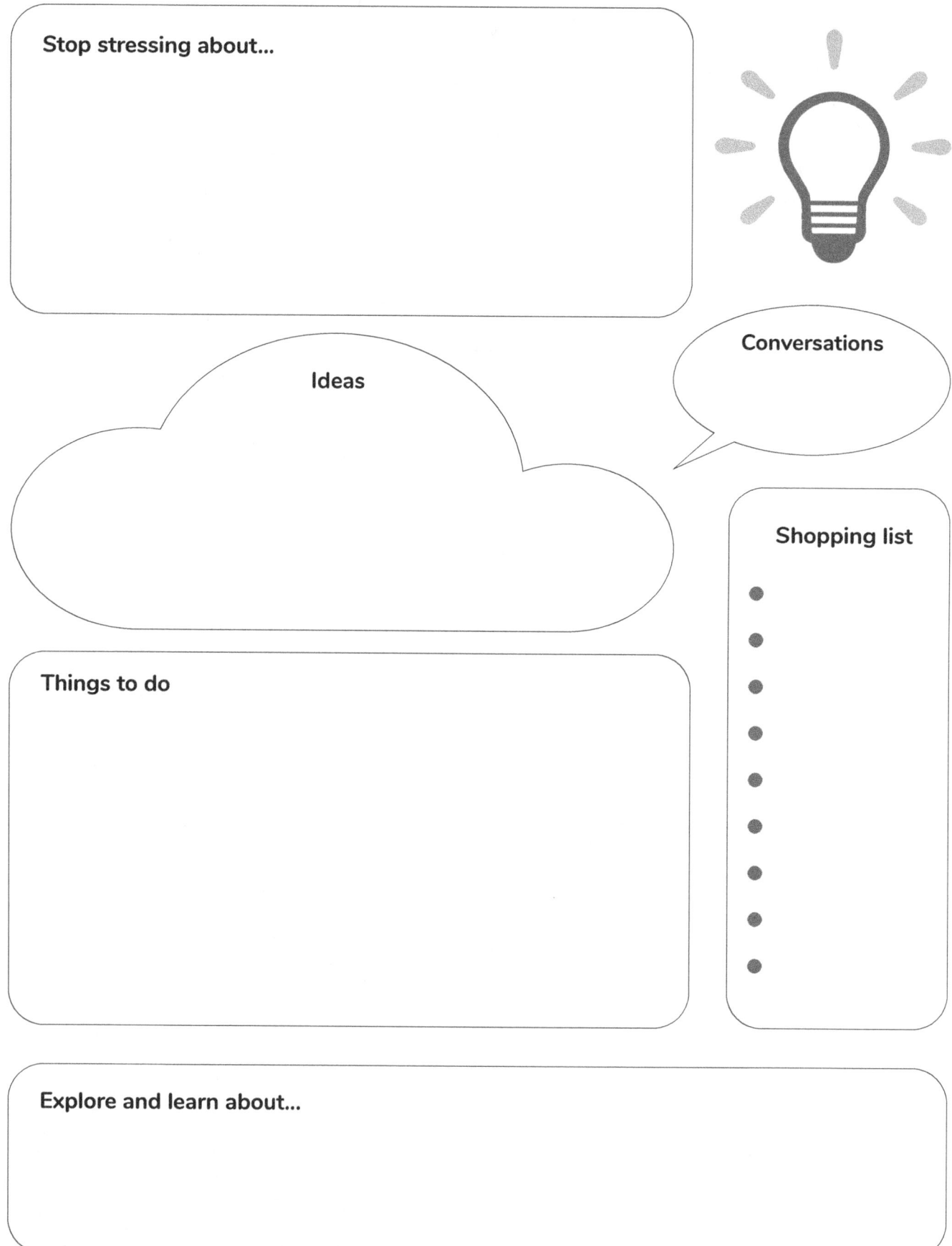

Ideas

Conversations

Shopping list
-
-
-
-
-
-
-
-
-

Things to do

Explore and learn about...

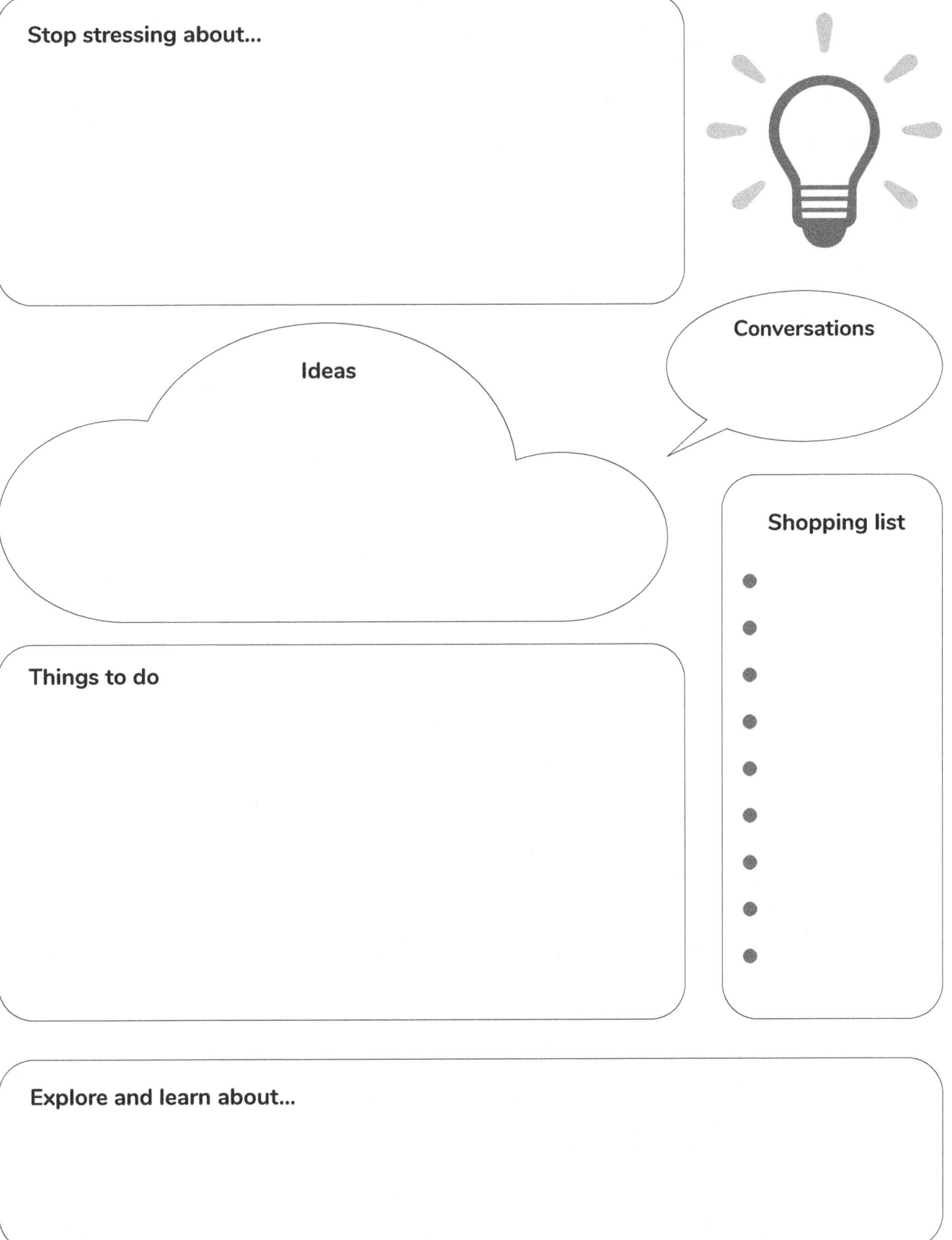

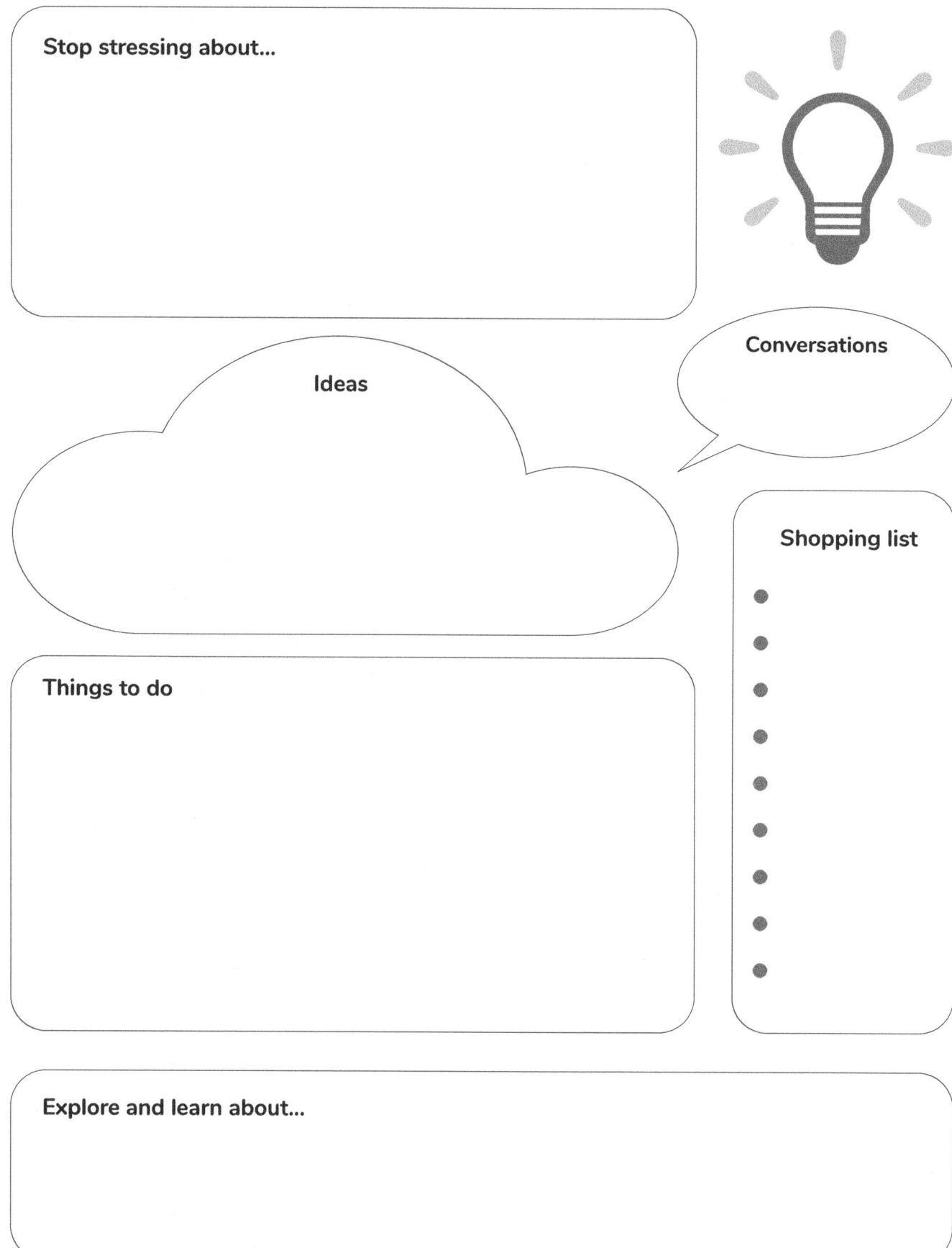

Stop stressing about...

Ideas

Conversations

Shopping list
-
-
-
-
-
-
-
-
-

Things to do

Explore and learn about...

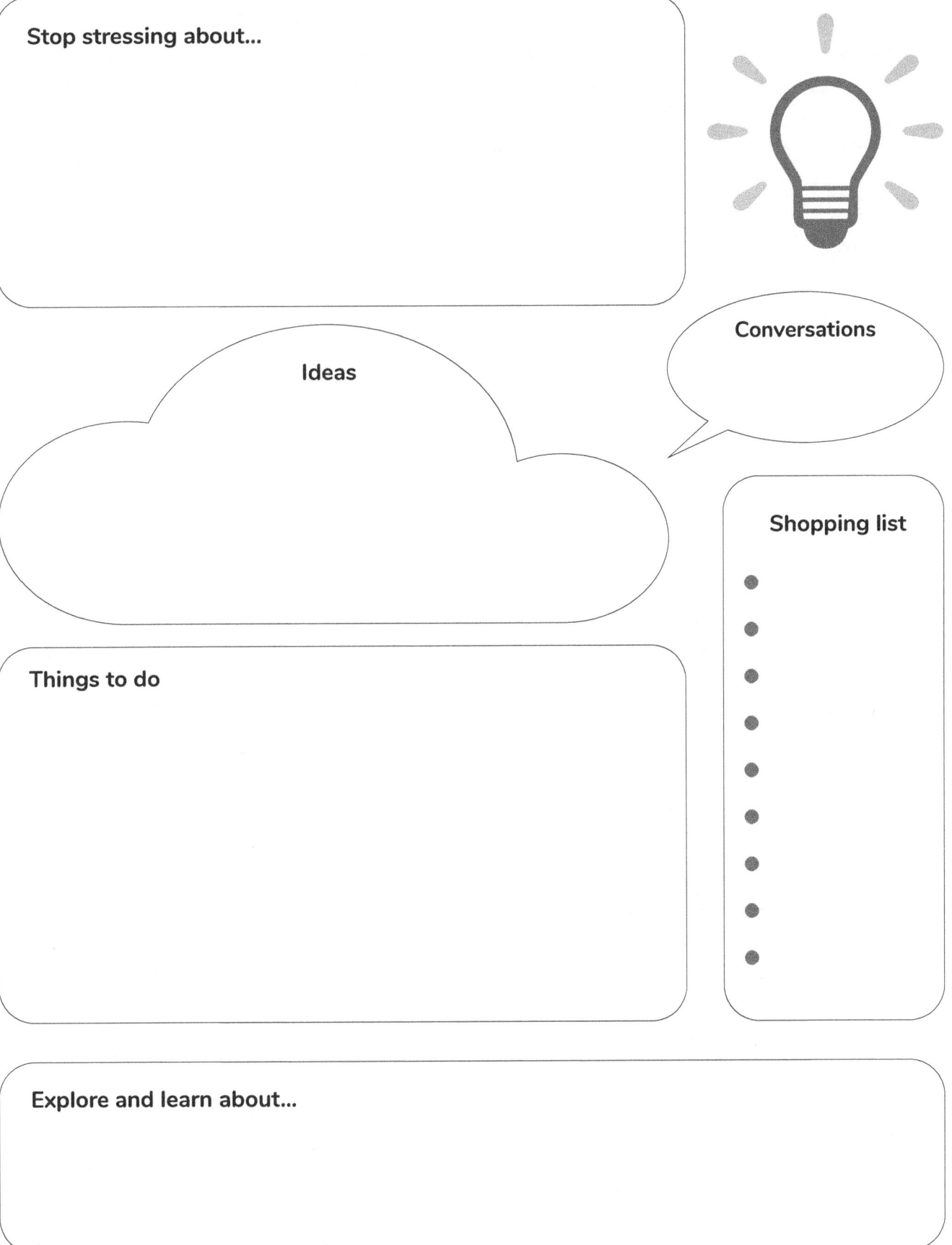

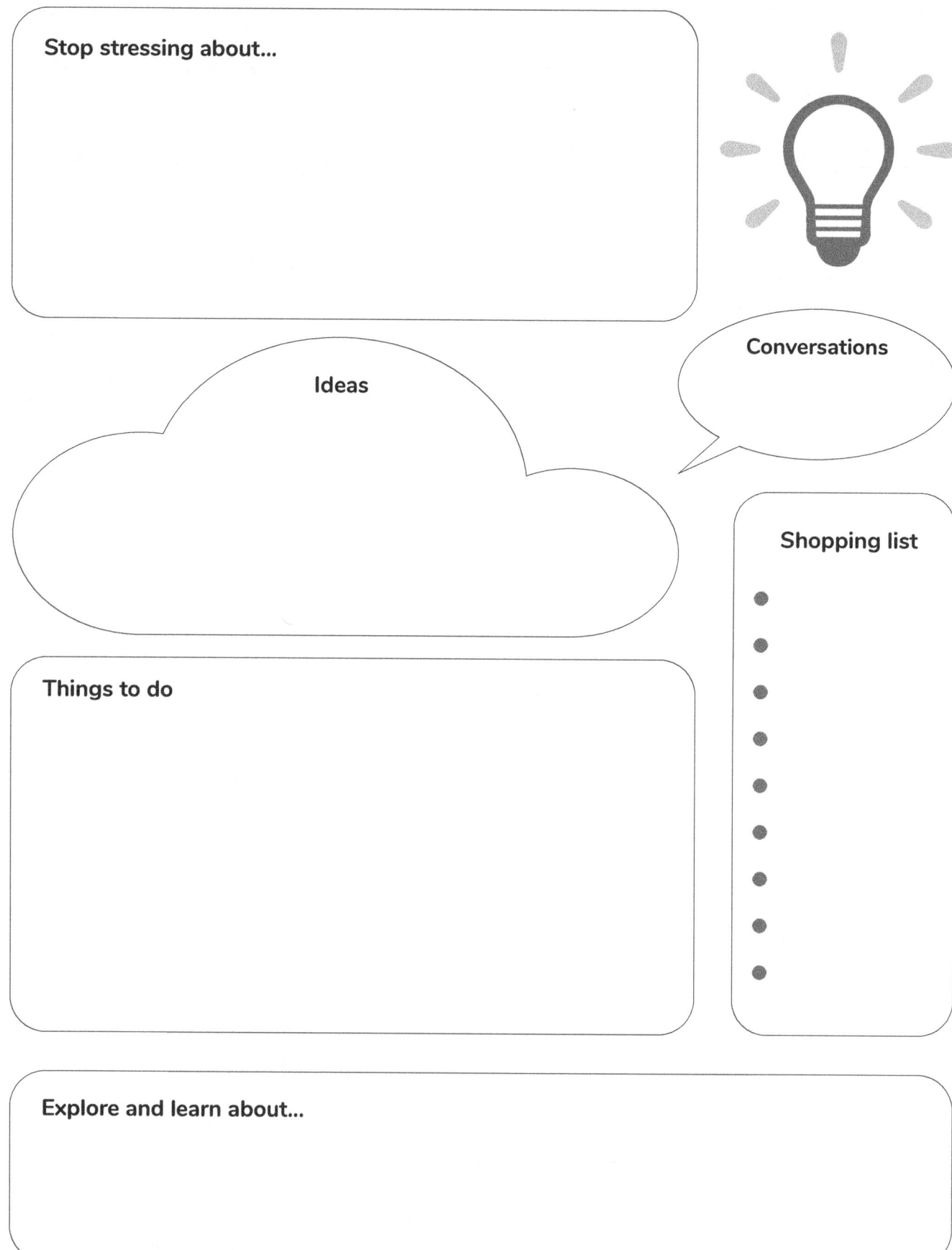

Stop stressing about...

Ideas

Conversations

Shopping list
-
-
-
-
-
-
-
-
-

Things to do

Explore and learn about...

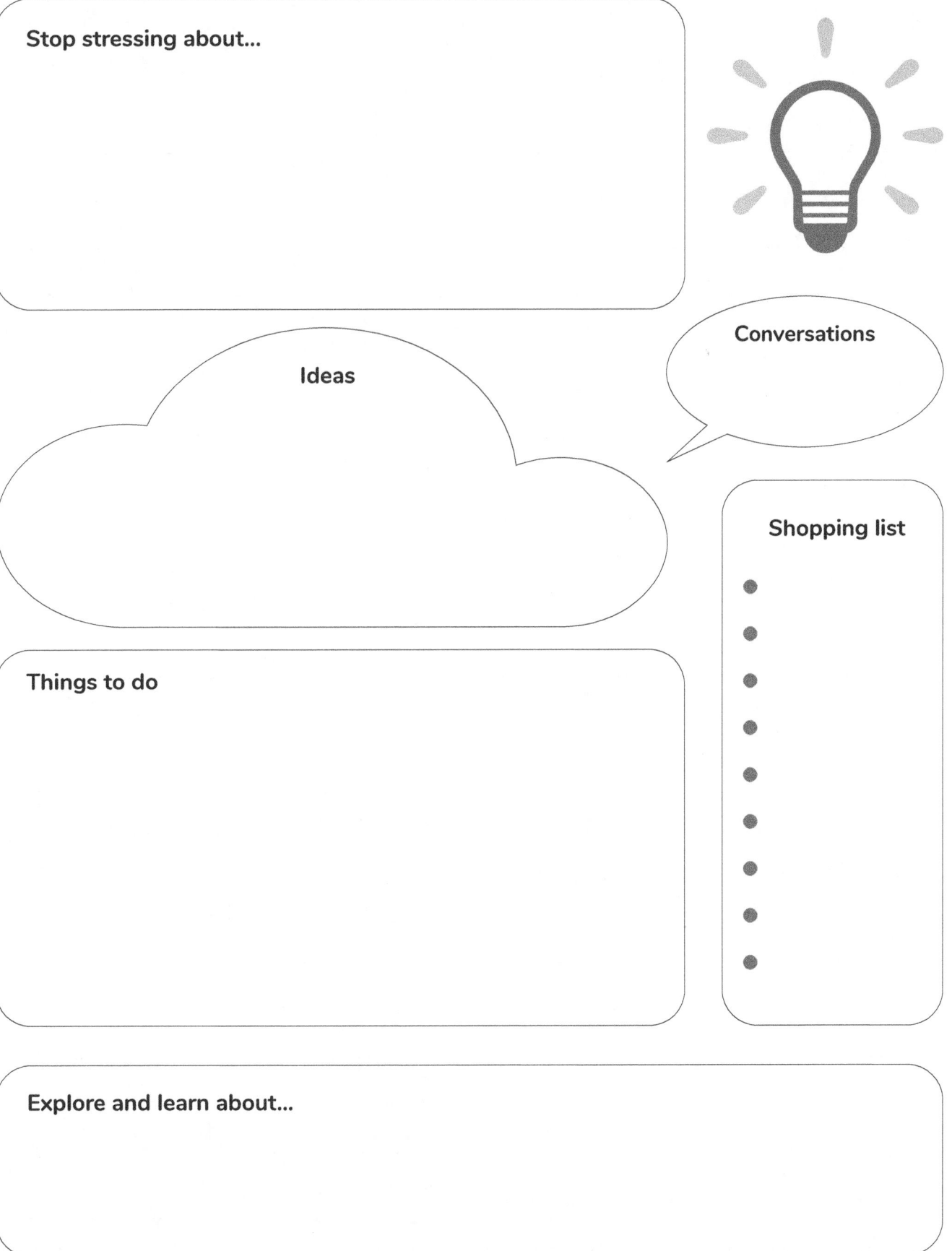

Stop stressing about...

Ideas

Conversations

Shopping list
-
-
-
-
-
-
-
-
-

Things to do

Explore and learn about...

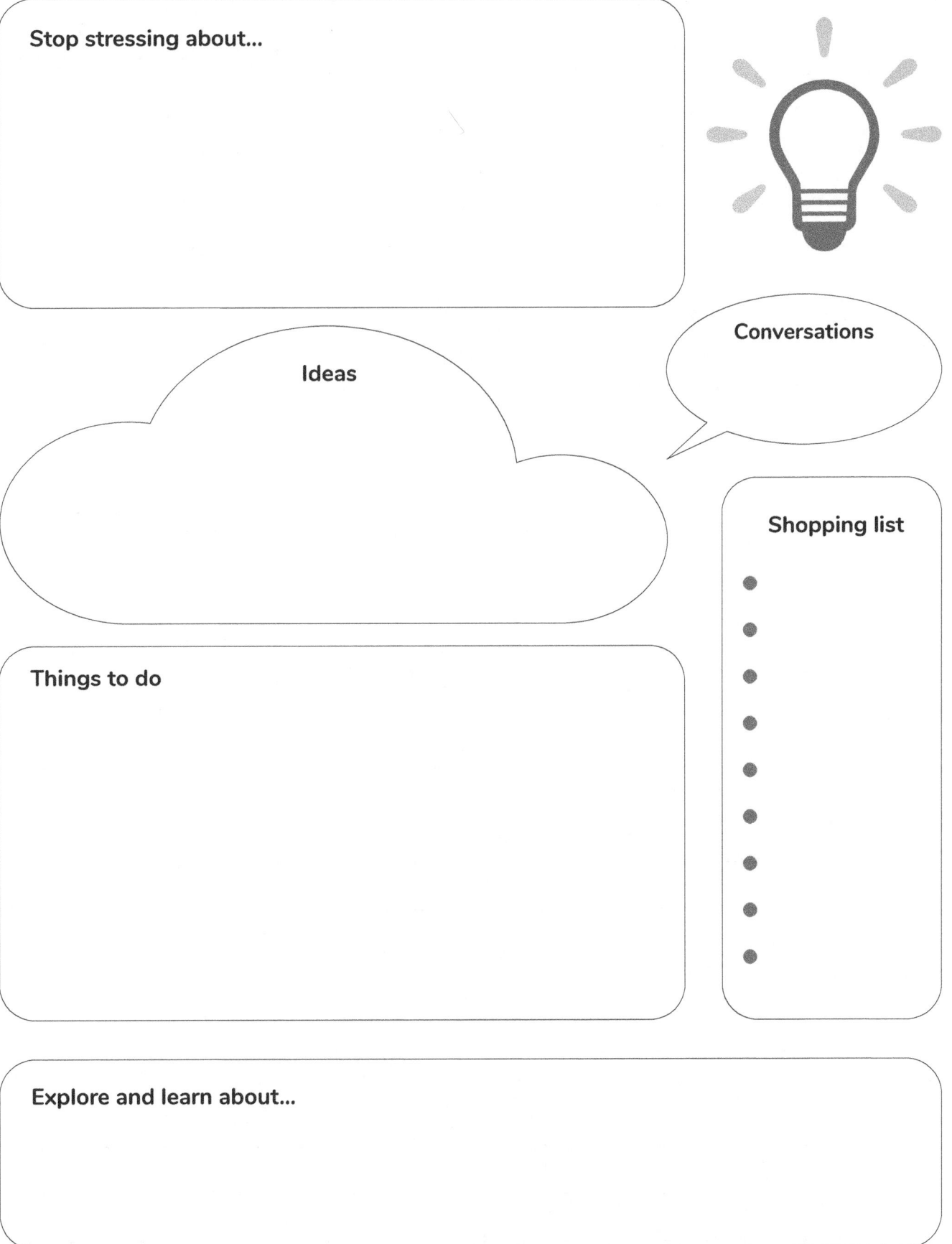

Stop stressing about...

Ideas

Conversations

Things to do

Shopping list
-
-
-
-
-
-
-
-
-

Explore and learn about...

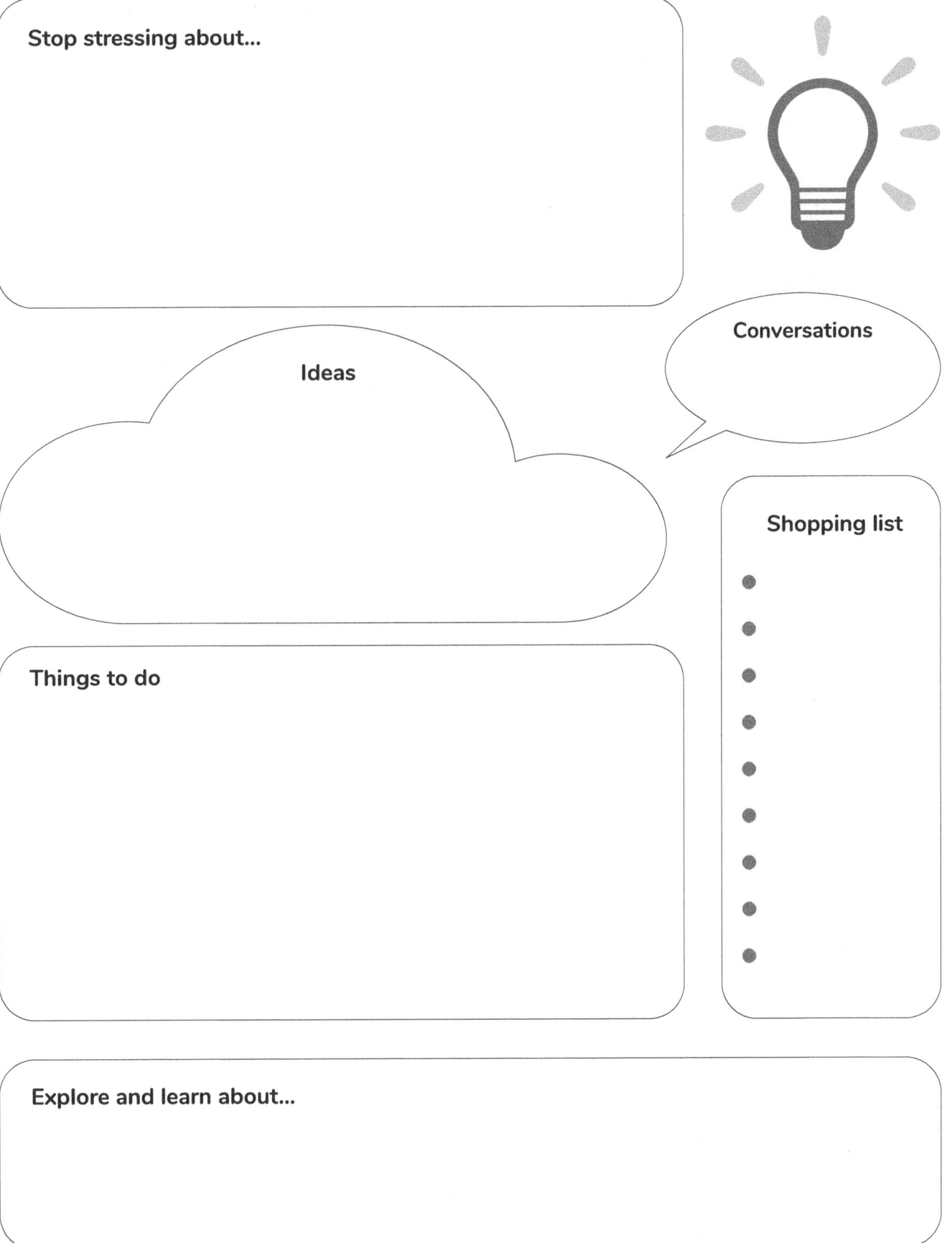

Stop stressing about...

Ideas

Conversations

Shopping list

-
-
-
-
-
-
-
-
-

Things to do

Explore and learn about...

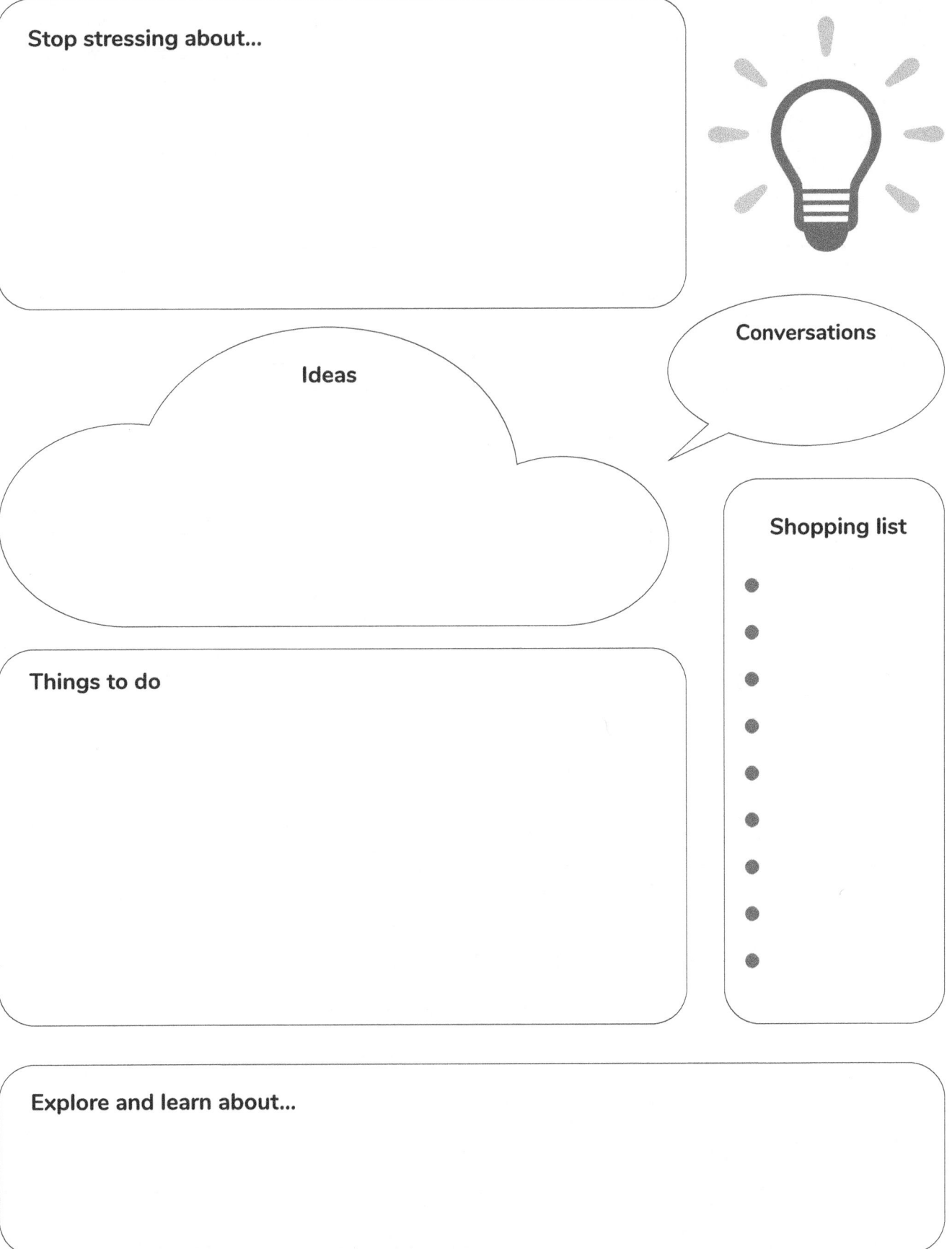

Stop stressing about...

Ideas

Conversations

Things to do

Shopping list

-
-
-
-
-
-
-
-
-

Explore and learn about...

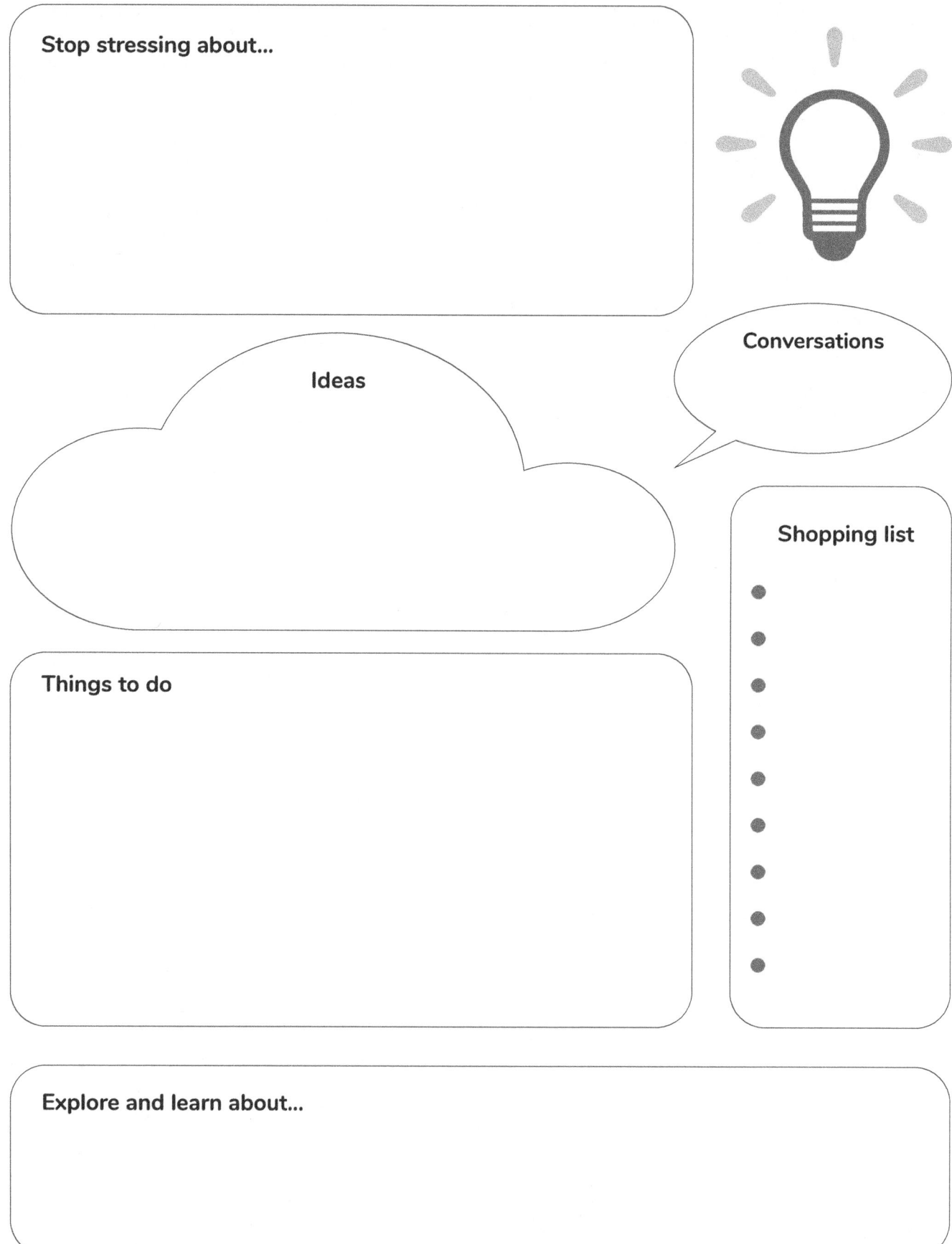

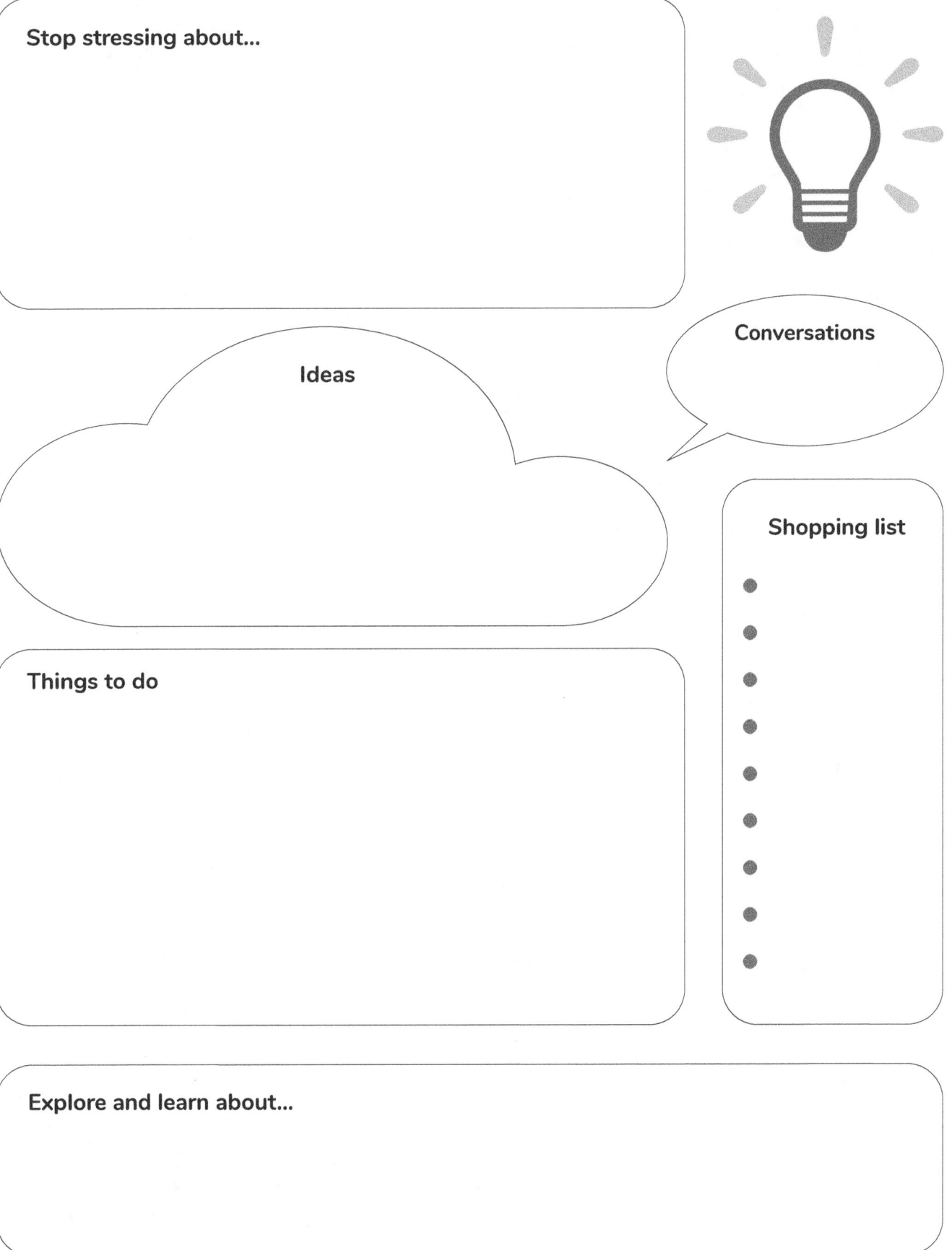

Stop stressing about...

Ideas

Conversations

Shopping list
-
-
-
-
-
-
-
-
-

Things to do

Explore and learn about...

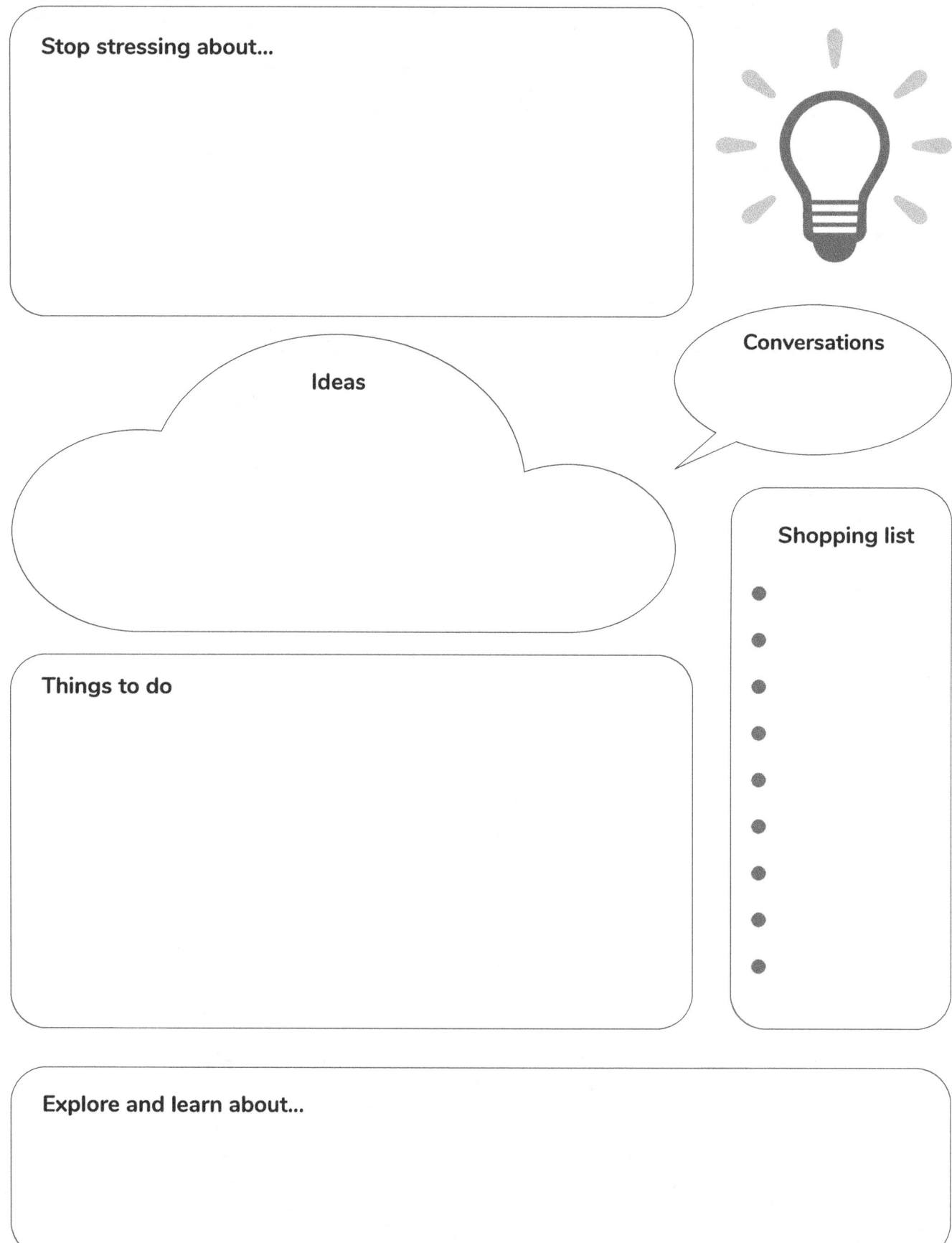

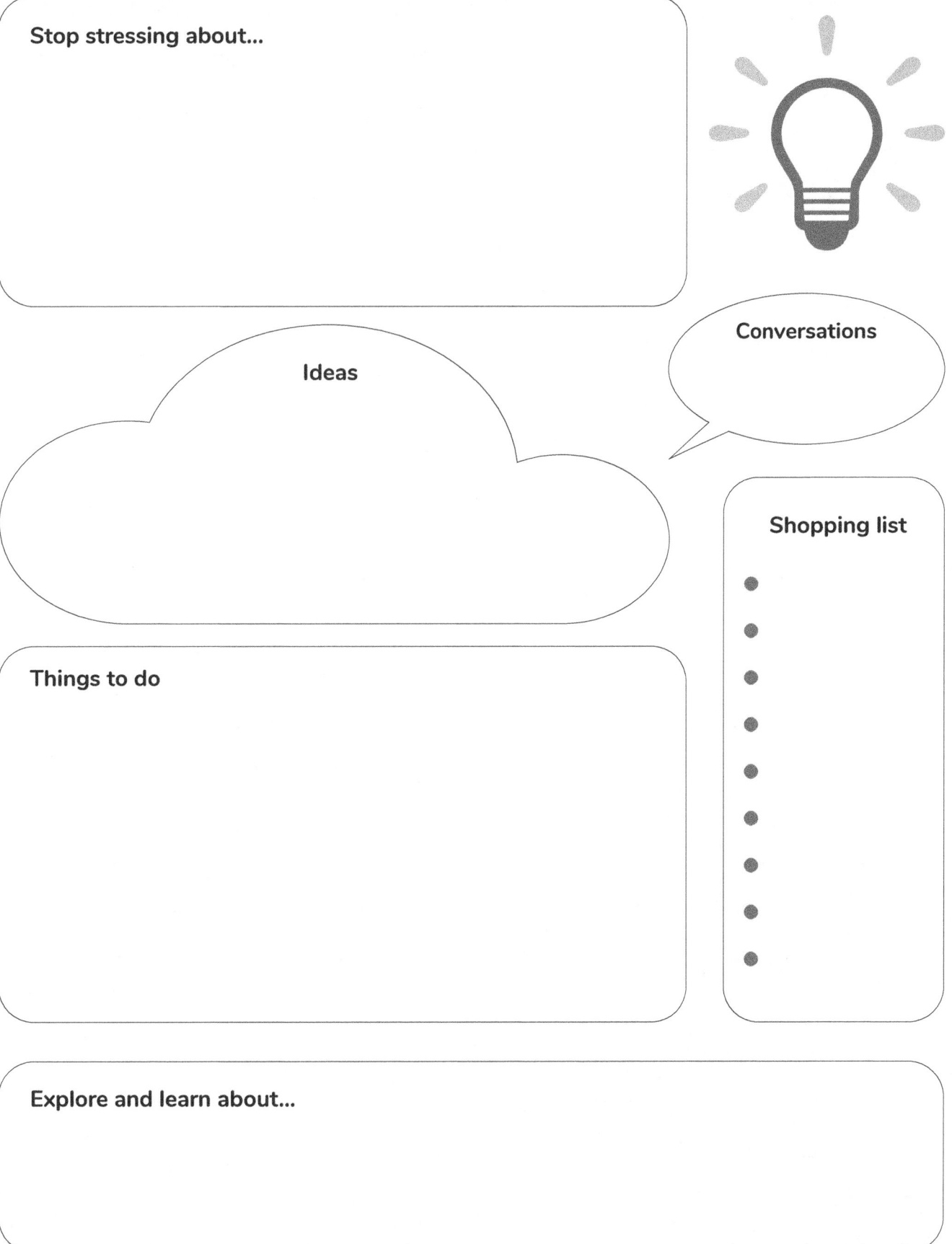

Stop stressing about...

Ideas

Conversations

Shopping list
-
-
-
-
-
-
-
-
-

Things to do

Explore and learn about...

Stop stressing about...

Ideas

Conversations

Shopping list
-
-
-
-
-
-
-
-
-

Things to do

Explore and learn about...

Stop stressing about...

Ideas

Conversations

Shopping list
-
-
-
-
-
-
-
-
-

Things to do

Explore and learn about...

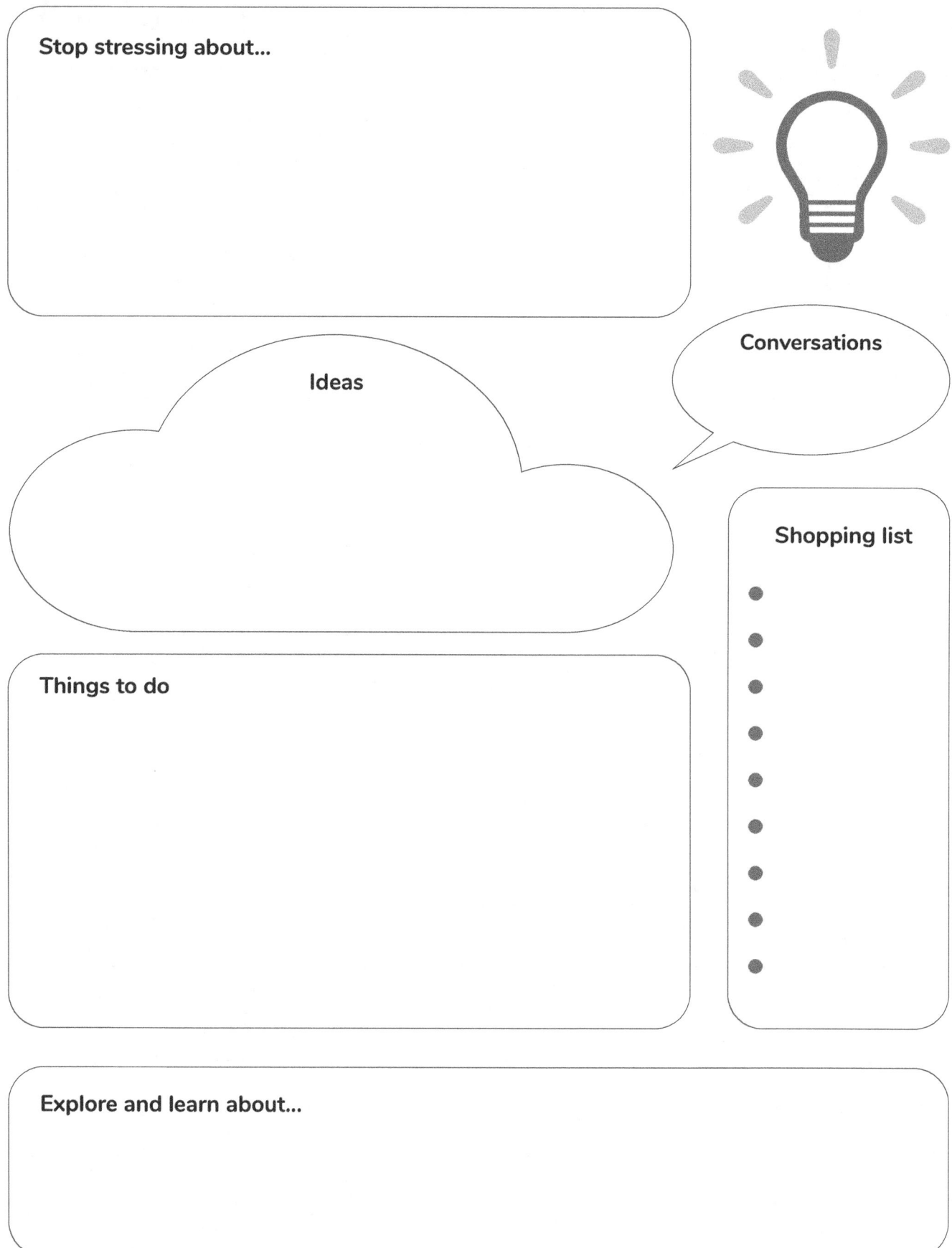

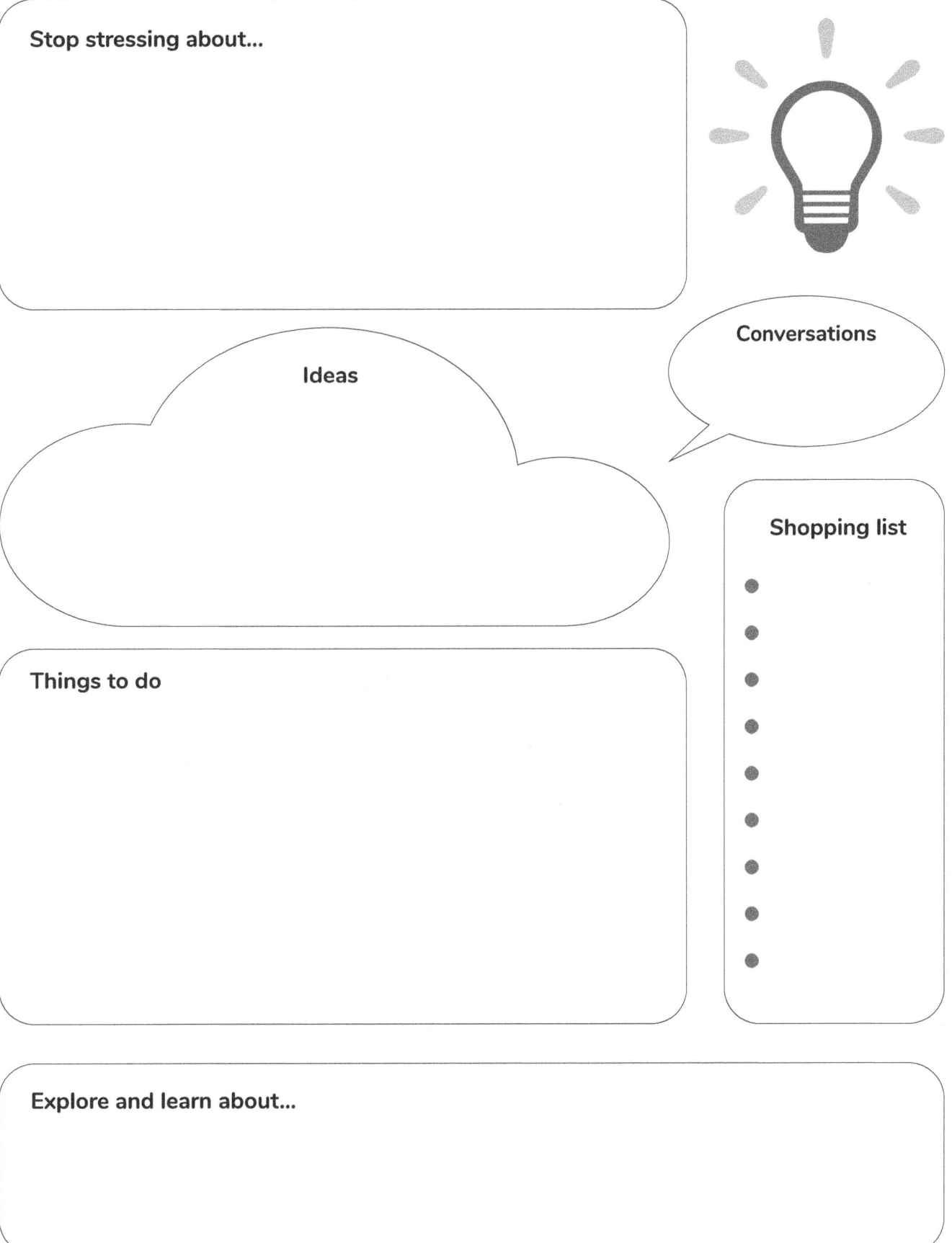

Stop stressing about...

Ideas

Conversations

Shopping list
-
-
-
-
-
-
-
-
-
-

Things to do

Explore and learn about...

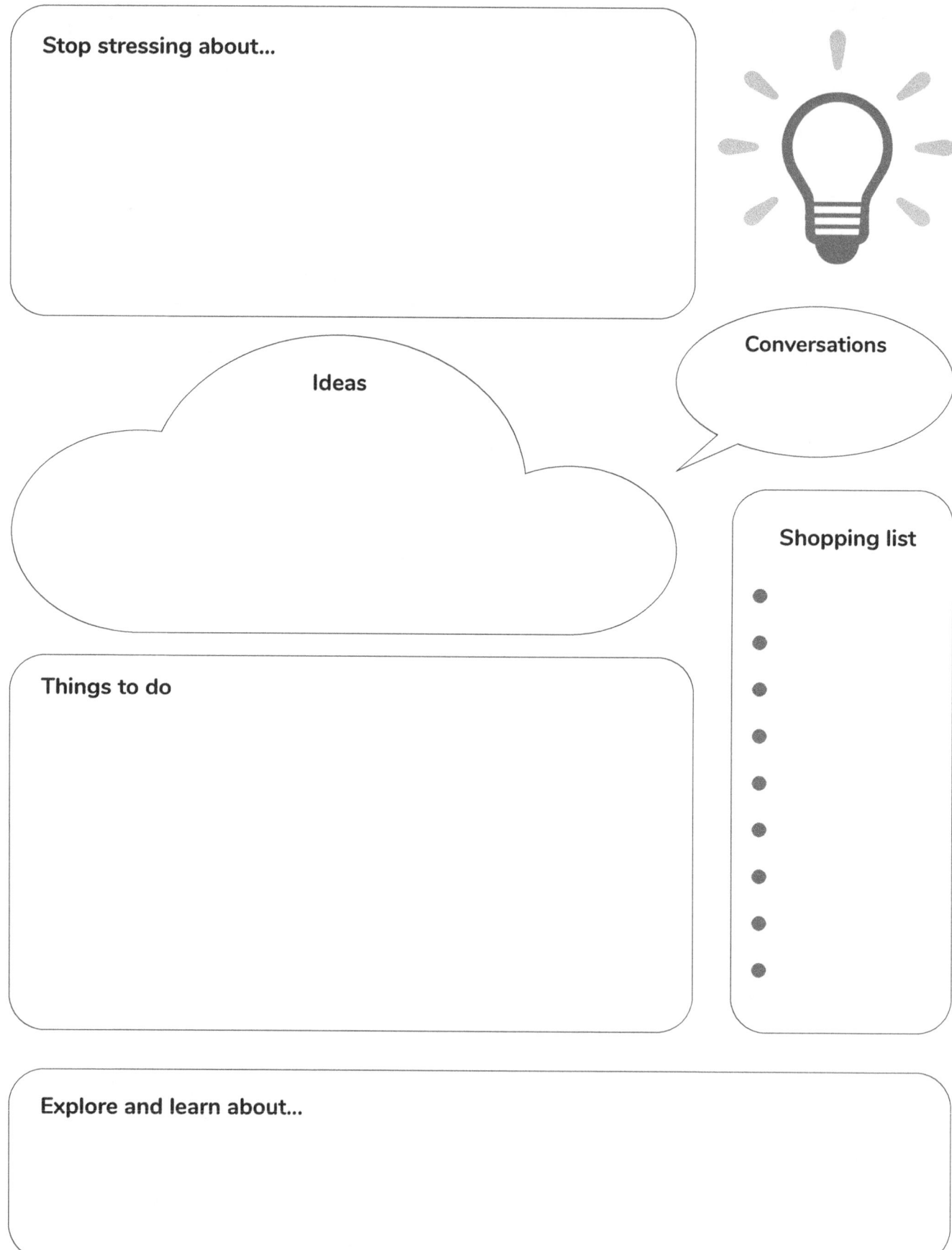

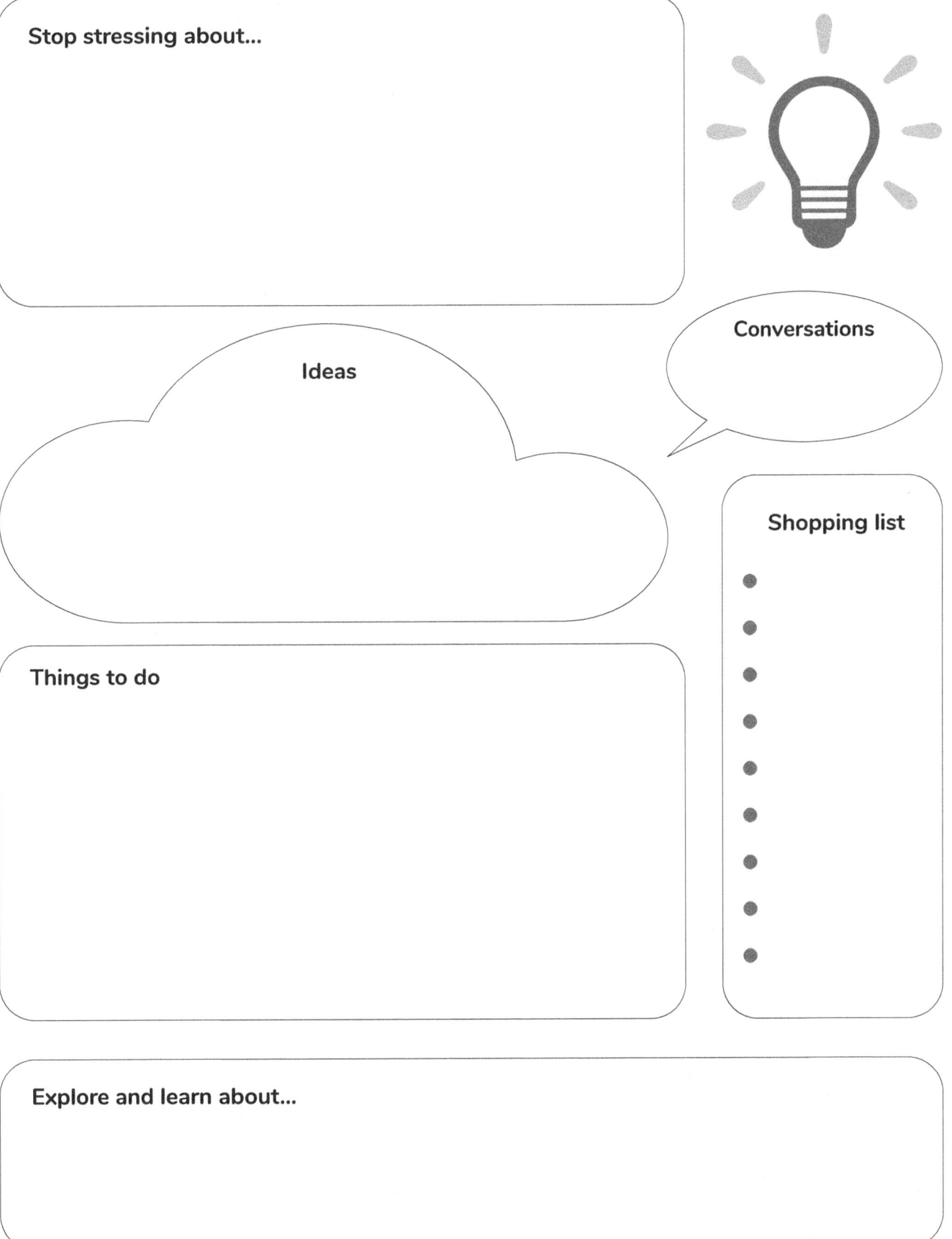

www.ingramcontent.com/pod-product-compliance
Lightning Source LLC
Chambersburg PA
CBHW081231080526
44587CB00022B/3894